Lent

Proclamation 4

Aids for Interpreting
the Lessons of the Church Year

Lent

Robert Hughes

Series A

FORTRESS PRESS   **MINNEAPOLIS**

PROCLAMATION 4
Aids for Interpreting the Lessons of the Church Year
Series A: Lent

Library of Congress Cataloging-in-Publication Data

(Revised for vol. 1–3, Series A)

Proclamation 4.

Consists of 24 volumes in 3 series designated A, B, and C, which correspond to the cycles of the three year lectionary. Each series contains 8 basic volumes with the following titles: [1] Advent-Christmas, [2] Epiphany, [3] Lent, [4] Holy Week, [5] Easter, [6] Pentecost 1, [7] Pentecost 2, and [8] Pentecost 3. (In addition there are four volumes on the lesser festivals.)
  By Christopher R. Seitz and others.
  Includes bibliographies.
  1. Bible—Liturgical lessons, English. 2. Bible—
Homiletical use. 3. Bible—Criticism, interpretation,
etc. 4. Common lectionary. 5. Church year. I. Seitz,
Christopher R. II. Title: Proclamation four.
BS391.2.S37 1988   264'.34   88–10982
ISBN 0-8006-4163-9 (Series A, Lent).

Manufactured in the U.S.A.   AF 1–4163

93   92   91   90   89   1   2   3   4   5   6   7   8   9   10

Contents

Ash Wednesday

Lutheran	Roman Catholic	Episcopal	Common Lectionary
Joel 2:12–19	Joel. 2:12–18	Joel 2:1–2, 12–17	Joel 2:1–2, 12–17a
2 Cor. 5:20b—6:2	2 Cor. 5:20—6:2	2 Cor. 5:20b—6:10	2 Cor. 5:20b—6:2 (3–10)
Matt. 6:1–6, 16–21	Matt. 6:1–6, 16–18	Matt. 6:1–6, 16–21	Matt. 6:1–6, 16–21

Many Christians mark this first day of the penitential season of Lent with reflection and self-examination, leading in some churches to a confession of sins. These lessons enable the preacher to make the connection between the biblical call to repentance and the good news of God's acceptance of separated sinners.

FIRST LESSON: JOEL 2:1–2, 12–19

What is known of Joel is what he says of himself; he is "the son of Pethuel" (1:1). From his use of the works of prior prophets and from the references in the book itself, scholars believe that Joel lived in Judah during the Persian period (539–331 B.C.). He was active between 400 and 350 B.C.

His interest in the temple and its liturgy has led scholars to the conclusion that Joel was a cultic prophet, one who ministered within the temple. Nevertheless, at the same time as Joel used classical themes and forms, his oracles are charged with a surprising apocalyptic fervor.

For Joel, the eschatological expectation of judgment comes to focus in the motif of the day of the Lord, a day of doom when God will deal with Israel and the Gentiles alike. The nearness of this end adds emotion and urgency to Joel's writing. In an apocalyptic mode, natural events or events of history can be portents of God's judgment. Flood and fire are images of the approaching horror.

The context of this reading is Joel's interpretation of a plague of locusts which laid waste the crops as God's judgment on the people and as a call to repentance (1:2—2:27). The plague was seen by the prophet as a portent of the coming day of the Lord, "a day of darkness and gloom" (2:2). Joel was definite about the meaning of the sign—God was angry because the people had been unfaithful. The appropriate response was repentance.

Christian preachers will recognize a potential discontinuity between this Old Testament text and the broad New Testament witness. Jesus himself was reluctant to ascribe "natural calamity" to God's retribution for human sin. In Luke 13:1–5 the common Semitic connection between sin and suffering is presumed, and Jesus did not argue for a disconnection. Rather, he resisted the link of specific sins and specific instances of suffering, while calling for the response of repentance. The saying recorded in Matt. 5:45 goes further in disconnecting sin and goodness from both suffering and blessing.

Several famous novelists have explored the link of "natural calamity" and suffering. Thornton Wilder's The *Bridge of San Luis Rey* recounts the struggle of Brother Juniper to come to grips intellectually with the deaths of five travelers, hurled into the gorge below when the famous Peruvian bridge collapsed. In *The Plague* by Albert Camus, dead rats in the streets and homes of Oran, Algeria, signal the onset of a disease that devastates the city. A wrenching subplot in the novel is Father Paneloux's struggle to understand the meaning of this pestilence. Initially, Paneloux preaches a sermon in which the plague is labeled God's retribution. Later, as he watches a boy die, Paneloux finds no sin heinous enough to merit this horrible death. Paneloux himself dies a bewildered man.

Pastors and laity alike experience the confusion of Paneloux as well as Brother Juniper's struggle to intellectualize suffering in hospital rooms and beside open graves. These contemporary instances of struggle with the meaning of suffering are resources for proclamation that will connect strongly with sensitive listeners.

In the face of a disastrous locust plague, Joel identifies repentance as a gift of God to avert total calamity (2:12–14). Joel's mention of fasting is a potential link to the appointed Gospel lesson.

Joel lampoons superficial signs of repentance. True repentance is marked by a thoroughgoing change of "hearts" rather than a superficial rending of "garments" (v. 13a). Undoubtedly, the contemporary practice of imposing ashes has the potential to mark a deep, inner change, although it may just as easily degenerate into an empty sign (see the discussion of Matthew 6). A focusing sentence for sermon preparation might be: In the face of unexplained suffering, through the word of contemporary prophets, questioning believers are called to return to God, their only source of help.

In Joel 2 both the gracious nature of God and the assurance of a better future are advanced as motives to respond. Joel proclaims that God is "gracious and merciful, slow to anger and abounding in steadfast love" (v. 13). The further good news is that, in response to their prayers, the gracious God "had pity" on the people and the plague was ended (vv. 18–19).

Liturgically speaking, penitential acts are remembrances of Baptism, the seminal event of repentance, cleansing, and renewal. In churches where a formal confession of sins is included in Ash Wednesday worship, the preacher may choose to underscore this link in the sermon: Penitents are called by a gracious God to remember their baptisms, so that washed and accepted, they are strengthened to live new lives.

SECOND LESSON: 2 CORINTHIANS 5:20b—6:2 (3–10)

Volumes have been written on the unity of 2 Corinthians, on the relationship between this epistle and what is called 1 Corinthians, and on the chronology of Paul's visits to Corinth and his correspondence (extant and lost) with that congregation. The position taken here is that between 1 and 2 Corinthians Paul made a "painful visit" (2:1) to Corinth and, in the aftermath, wrote a severe letter (which we do not possess) "out of much affliction and anguish of heart and with many tears" (2:4). He sent this letter to Corinth with Titus, the person to whom he had given responsibility to restore order in the congregation. Upon receipt of the letter a positive change took place in Corinth, with the majority of the members repenting of their insubordinate behavior. When Paul heard this news from Titus he was filled with joy and wrote the bulk of our 2 Corinthians.

This Ash Wednesday reading is part of 2:4—7:4, Paul's apology for his apostleship and ministry in Corinth in the face of his detractors. Paul's polemical defense appears to move on three levels. First, Paul opposes a protognostic interpretation of the Christian message similar in many ways to the "theology of glory" engaged in 1 Corinthians. In addition, Paul does battle against "prophets" from Palestine who have challenged his credentials, his apostleship, and his gospel. They are proud of their Jewish origins (11:22), but Paul denounces them as servants of Satan (11:13–15). Finally, at least one person in the congregation, who has attacked Paul personally (2:5–11; 7:12) and who has been disciplined, receives some comment.

However, despite the enmity that existed between Paul and some members of the Corinthian church, the focus of this reading is reconciliation between God and God's people. Paul appeals to his readers to "be reconciled to God" (5:20), that is, to accept God's forgiveness effected by Christ. God made the sinless Christ bear the burden of sin in order that sinful humans might be made righteous (5:21). Paul appeals to the Corinthians to respond to this free gift and to do so "now" (6:2).

The urgency of this response is rooted in Paul's conviction that the day of the Lord that Joel spoke about is in process of realization. The gift of reconciliation in Jesus Christ fulfills God's promise to establish a new reign of harmony.

It would be a mistake for the preacher to view reconciliation between God and God's creation as something essentially different from justification. While it is true that these metaphors are drawn from different areas of life, they point to the same reality—the need of humanity to be made right with God. The terms are used in parallelism in Rom. 5:9–10, and in the verse immediately preceding this reading reconciliation is described as God's "not counting their trespasses against them" (5:19).

Paul's employment of the metaphor of reconciliation makes it clear that human estrangement is overcome solely at God's initiative ("all this is from God, who through Christ reconciled us to himself," 5:18). Romans 5:11 speaks of reconciliation as something "received." In Paul's world view, humans are enslaved by the powers of an evil age and are unable to reconcile themselves to God. Therefore, when this pericope opens with the injunction "be reconciled to God" (5:20), it should be clear that the initiative, method, and motivation for reconciliation belong to God.

Inherent in the metaphor is the reality of estrangement from the creator ("while we were enemies we were reconciled to God," Rom. 5:10). History is a sad record of humans going their own way rather than God's way. Despite its superficial character development, F. Scott Fitzgerald's *The Great Gatsby* captures the flash and charisma of human striving, as well as its doomed end.

> Gatsby believed in the green light, the orgiastic future that year by year recedes before us. It eluded us then, but that's no matter—tomorrow we will run faster, stretch out our arms farther. . . . And one fine morning—
>
> So we beat on, boats against the current, borne back ceaselessly into the past.[1]

The separation of person from person and community from community occurs as a ripple effect of human estrangement from God, the ground of being. For Paul's application of reconciliation to the area of human relations, see 1 Cor. 7:11. While the preacher may be tempted to zero in on indifference to injustice, cruelty, prejudice, pride of race and class, and aggressive competition as examples of human estrangement, he or she should make clear that these are simultaneously symptoms and manifestations of the deeper fissure in the divine–human relationship.

Ash Wednesday is an excellent time for the preacher to underscore the reality of the entire Christian life as a dying and rising with Christ. A life of reconciliation with God, begun in the cross of Jesus Christ, personalized in baptism, is an ongoing process. Accepting the reconciliation offered by God requires penitence, not simply regret for deeds done or left undone, but a daily turning from sin to embrace God's grace. The sermon message may be summarized thus: To persons who experience estrangement from God (perhaps through human separation and hostility), God calls us NOW to accept the new relationship offered to estranged human beings.

GOSPEL: MATTHEW 6:1–6, 16–21

Internal evidence suggests that the destruction of the temple (A.D. 70) had occurred by the time the Gospel attributed to St. Matthew was written. The Markan tradition was known by the evangelist, but it had undergone some changes by the time he utilized it. Tensions between Jews and Christians are apparent in the Gospel, and there is evidence to suggest that these groups had begun to worship separately. However, widespread persecution of Christians is not suggested by the evidence. Indeed, while attempting to distinguish between Jewish and Christian piety in this unit and elsewhere in the Gospel the writer of Matthew seems determined to maintain the continuity between the traditions. All of this suggests a dating for Matthew of A.D. 85–89.

Contextually, this passage is part of Matthew 5:1—7:29, the so–called Sermon on the Mount. After retaining the Markan narrative structure in chaps. 3–4, Matthew inserts this teaching section, only to pick up the Markan account again in chaps. 8–28.

One source lying behind Matthew 5–7 is abbreviated as Q. This collection of Jesus' teachings, probably employed by the early church in the catechetical instruction of converts preparing for baptism, stands in a direct line with such documents as Proverbs and the Wisdom of Solomon. In Q Jesus is presented as Messiah in message as well as actions.

Matthew takes pains to support the continued authority of Pharisaic teaching while articulating a theology for the new church. In chap. 6 the evangelist wrestles with the meaning for Christians of the three most important demonstrations of religious devotion in Judaism (Tob. 12:8; cf. Acts 10:31).

Eduard Schweizer believes that three "radical" sayings of Jesus lie behind the present passage.[2] Although we cannot be certain precisely what they were, he contends that all three rule out achievement in the eyes of God. Schweizer and other commentators suggest that the Christian community combined these sayings while toning them down as a response to questions of new converts about the relevance of Jewish devotional practices for Christians. The writer of Matthew includes this unit of teaching in his Gospel in order to give his Jewish-Christian community guidance about living both within and over against its tradition.

The literary unity of the passage is signaled by a repetition of key words and phrases. When read aloud in worship this parallel construction is noted by listeners. What the "hypocrites" do in terms of almsgiving, prayer, and fasting is contrasted with the attitude and behavior of Christians.

Someone, either the writer of Matthew or an editor, broke the unity of the three sayings yoked together in the oral tradition. By focusing on the theme of prayer, this person was able to insert vv. 7–15. As a result, important teachings on prayer were preserved, including the Lord's Prayer, but the insertion fractured the unit. Most lectionaries restore the connection so the reading itself is a unity.

The parallelism of words and phrases is a clue to the preacher that the historical linkage of sayings on almsgiving, prayer, and fasting is possible for preaching purposes. A strong unifying element is the contrast between a "secret" devotion addressed to God (6:3–4, 6, 17, 18) and a "public" devotion done in the sight of all. The repetition of "secret" (six times) and "seen (or praised) by men" (three times) underscores the contrast for listeners. Those who perform religious duties for human consumption are "hypocrites" who have received their reward already, while those who do the secret devotion have a reward coming from God.

In classical Greek the term "hypocrite" *(hypokritēs,* 6:2, 5, 16) meant only "play actor," one who takes a role.

However, the Aramaic language added the connotation of "profane person." Matthew uses the word fourteen times, usually of the Pharisees, in the negative sense of pretending to be pious or virtuous without really being so.

In 6:1 the term "righteousness" *(dikaiosunē)* is translated variously as "alms" (KJV), "religion" (NEB), and "piety" (RSV). Broadly, the reference is to the performance of religious duties (see Tob. 12:9). While alms and piety are fuzzy terms seldom used with precision today, a focus on the performance of religious obligations and ceremonies immediately suggests a number of applications.

On the surface, Matthew 6 seems to prohibit any outward display ("Be careful not to perform your religious duties in public"). However, central to the text is the contrast between "so that people will see what you do" and "in secret" (for God's eyes only). Outward religious displays are *not* prohibited by this passage; rather, the prohibition targets the motive behind the action. Anything done to win the attention or esteem of others is performed for the wrong reason.

The practice of the imposition of ashes, standard on Ash Wednesday in the Roman Catholic tradition, is spreading among other Christian groups. Imposing ashes as a sign of repentance is an ancient biblical practice (e.g., Jon. 3:5–9, Job 42:6; Jer. 6:26, Matt. 11:21) adopted by Christians as an outward mark of an inner disposition. Ashes remind the individual who receives them of God's condemnation of sin and its link to human mortality (Gen. 3:19). At the same time, in the absence of soap, ancients used ashes for cleansing. Imposed in the form of a cross, the ashen mark looks backward over the history of human sin and ahead to God's redemptive event on Good Friday. Pastors of churches that impose ashes will do well to interpret this and other Lenten practices in the light of Matthew 6. This sentence may assist the preacher to focus: People who engage in religious practices to make a show of their piety are reminded that true devotion is directed entirely to God, who, through the cross of Jesus Christ, saves believers from sin and death.

Note that the contrast explicit in the text suggests that the sermon shape itself as a contrast. The preacher may begin with the obvious dangers of outward show, holding the "good news" message of cleansing, renewal, and the cross for the second half of the sermon.

Some preachers will be pastors of churches where special financial gifts to the congregation or other denominational causes is made a Lenten discipline for members. So-called self-denial offerings remain a common form of fund raising in this penitential season. Where donations to the church are concerned, the Matthean warning against outward show and the focus on purer motives (no one's motives are ever pure) is appropriate.

Biblical commentators note that in the temple there were six trumpet-shaped receptacles for depositing alms. At one time trumpets may have been sounded to call attention to major gifts, but the injunction to "sound no trumpet" (v. 2) is probably a figure of speech in this text. Schweizer translates the Greek as "do not make a big show of it."

Published lists of donors and donations, brass plaques on memorial gifts, and books with donor amounts listed are devices the church has borrowed from the world to let people see what we do. If the operative motive is to witness to God's generosity while modeling a response of thanksgiving for other believers, these and other practices may be worthy. If the motive is to "make a big show of it," evoking pride in the giver and guilt in the observer, then such methods are inappropriate. Matthew 6:3 calls for what is humanly impossible but spiritually preferable, namely, "Do not let your left hand know what your right hand does." Test this summary sentence against the thrust of the reading: Congregations who desire to make a big show of giving are warned against marking and measuring contributions and are called, before God, to give unknowingly.

Another possible sermon focus is the devotional practice of prayer (6:5–6). Unison prayer in the temple was practiced alongside of private prayer. Fixed times of prayer had developed by the time Matthew was written and were observed by turning to face the temple in Jerusalem. Prayers were said aloud only during public fasts; otherwise they were whispered. Matthew 6 recommends withdrawing from public view for prayer. The text mentions, suggestively and metaphorically, seeking privacy in the small storage room attached to a house. Devotion to God is not for public recognition (see Luke 18:10–14).

A sermon on fasting may receive a new hearing in the midst of a culture where persons are concerned about health and often obsessed with a desire to lose weight. However, "making a big show" of three trips a week to the spa, a tuned body, and participation in the latest fad diet is prideful. Flexed biceps and expressions of hunger designed to win attention and admiration are childish.

Fasting may have something to commend it in Lent if the devotion is both hidden and joyous. In fact, Jesus told his disciples not to fast while he was with them. True repentance (like almsgiving and prayer) is a joy, an anticipation of the kingdom (Mark 2:19; Matt. 9:15). The practice is its own reward. A laudable social dimension of fasting and so-called hunger meals is an identification with those here and around the world who go hungry to bed. If money saved on food is donated to local soup kitchens for the poor and homeless, or to the world hunger appeal, so much the better. Try this sermon sentence: Jesus reminds us, when we tend to show off our piety, that true repentance is a joyful event rooted in God's goodness.

Three common errors are displayed in published sermons on this text. The first, as suggested, is to focus on the religious actions rather than on the motivation for doing them and on God before whom they are done.

The second is to suggest that Judaism was guilty of hypocrisy whereas Christian religious practices were and are genuine. In fact, alongside the formal catechetical use, the writer of Matthew may have inserted this bit of early teaching-preaching to counter hypocrisy in the religious life of his own community.

The final error is to preach this text only as prohibition and restriction. For a Jewish-Christian group struggling with its identity, Jesus gives an assuring message of a higher righteousness that does not need to credit works of piety and is oblivious to personal acclaim. There are many congregations today, both new and established, struggling to find themselves and to forge an identity, for whom a dispensation from crediting achievements goes to the very heart of the gospel. In sum: To insecure Christians struggling to discover who they are, Jesus comes in his word reassuring them that they are acceptable apart from what they do.

The First Sunday in Lent

Lutheran	Roman Catholic	Episcopal	Common Lectionary
Gen. 2:7–9, 15–17, 3:1–7	Gen. 2:7–9, 3:1–7	Gen. 2:4b–9, 15–17, 25—3:7	Gen. 2:4b–9, 15–17, 25—3:7
Rom. 5:12, 17–19	Rom. 5:12–19	Rom. 5:12–19	Rom. 5:12–19
Matt. 4:1–11	Matt. 4:1–11	Matt. 4:1–11	Matt. 4:1–11

The lessons for this day project a remarkable unity: Adam and Christ, fallen humanity and redeemed humanity, death and life, unfaithfulness and obedience. At the start of the Lenten journey, from the peak of the mount of temptation, we are able to see back to the garden and ahead to the cross.

FIRST LESSON: GENESIS 2:4b–9, 15–17; 3:1–7

This lection centers on the great themes of creation and fall. By dealing with both sin and its effects, it addresses the issue of why the creation is not as God intended and why it needed to be redeemed by Jesus Christ.

In terms of literary context, the Priestly account (P) of creation (1:1—2:4a) immediately precedes this narrative. The P account is the latest source in the Pentateuch, composed in the postexilic period, ca. 538–450 B.C.

However, the Yahwistic account (J) that begins with Genesis 2:4b is much older, dated ca. 950 B.C. While gaps in the story line and doublets (two trees) suggest that J was woven from several sources, there is no consensus about separating these in chaps. 2 and 3. Most scholars believe that the threads were combined prior to the work of the Yahwist (so-called because of his name for God). The use of the two designations Yahweh-Elohim in these chapters is apparently the work of a later redactor.

Theologically, Gen. 3:1–7 is the opening scene of what someone has called "the great hamartiology" of chaps. 3–11, the account of how sin broke into the world and spread like a plague. These stories are an account of the rebellion of the creatures against the Creator and of how God reacted. After each incident of disobedience, along with increasingly severe punishments, God's will to save is revealed. Only the final narrative, the account of the Tower of Babel (11:1–9), does not conclude with a word of grace. It does serve, nevertheless, as a backdrop for the beginning of "sacred history," the election of Abraham to begin a new nation and to be the channel of blessing for the world.

The Yahwistic account is narrative in form. The extended story is broken into individual scenes characterized both by simplicity of expression and maturity of theme. The early stories are highly anthropomorphic. God walks in the garden in the cool of the evening, gives specific instructions about Adam's diet, and later hand stitches clothing for the sinful pair. At the same time, this divine companion is the Creator of the universe who calls the creatures to account for their sinful desire "to be like God" (3:5). Evidently the Yahwist planned a complete primeval history to give his contemporaries insight into the ongoing saga of God and humans.

This Yahwistic account is strikingly different from the Priestly creation story. In chap. 1 humanity is the end and pinnacle of God's creative sequence; in chap. 2 the creation of the man is God's first action. The bond of life between earth and humanity is clear in the play on the Hebrew words *'adam* (humankind) and *'adamah* (ground) in v. 7. A bit of dust is animated by the divine breath, a vivid demonstration that life comes from God. God goes on to create a garden, animals, and woman to surround the man and make his joy complete. The creation of woman affirms both sexuality and community as good gifts of the Creator. Eden means "delight" and, in this account, Eden is not a mythological "garden of the gods" but a garden designed for the creatures' pleasure. By assigning the creatures to till the garden and keep it, God affirms that work is itself a gift (2:15).

The imposition of limitations on humanity foreshadows the crux of the narrative, the turning point at which the creature refuses to be bound by those limits. The introduction of a mythological "tree of life" (2:9), whose fruit upon eating grants immortality, is used by the Yahwist only to frame the narrative (3:24). However, a second tree, whose fruit yields a "knowledge of good and evil" (2:9), is crucial to the story. This tree of knowledge, whose fruit is incorrectly pictured in later interpretation as an apple, will be used in the serpent's temptation.

In mythology the serpent is a sinister power. However, in this narrative the serpent is a creature of God who embodies cleverness (3:1). The animal's ability to speak is a characteristic the Genesis story has in common with fable. In the hands of the Yahwist the talking snake assumes a secondary role, as the narrator focuses on the humans and their guilt.

The serpent cleverly draws the woman into conversation by distorting God's command, leading the woman in turn to exaggerate the divine limits (God didn't say, "Don't touch," 3:3). The serpent's insinuation that God withholds knowledge grudgingly, and the beast's claim that death will not result from eating the fruit, tempts the humans to exceed God's imposed limits (3:4–5). This human pair were not undernourished or deprived; they wanted more. The essence of their temptation is pride, seeking divine knowledge and power and being unwilling to be obedient creatures.

The preacher will note that the tendency of earlier commentators and theologians to make the woman more responsible for sin than the man distorts the intention of the narrative. Both are responsible. While the man does blame the woman (3:12), the narrator uses this "passing the buck" as a symptom of sin. It is interesting to observe that in Romans 5 Paul blames Adam and never mentions Eve.

One general truth this story tells is that some limitations are helpful and ignored only at great cost. The sign reads "Tow-away Zone." The woolen sweater is labeled, "Wash only in cold water." The bottle of pills indicates, "Take no more than four in any twenty-four-hour period." Limits can be helpful, but humans tend to press beyond them in ways that are harmful.

One theological message of this text is that God's plan for the world includes limits that we humans transgress repeatedly. For example, the Decalogue says, "Do not commit adultery," but we see husbands and wives who are courting the death of a relationship by reaching outside marriage for the alluring fruit of sexual freedom. The pattern of Adam and Eve is our own: limits, rebellion, death. For preaching, one could summarize: God gives life by imposing helpful limits on men and women, who sinfully seek to define life on their own terms.

In a culture dominated by humanistic psychology and its message of self-actualization, it is commonly asserted that self-realization is an unqualified good. The aim of the "me generation" seems to consist primarily in actualizing human potential and filling human needs of all kinds—emotional, sexual, and intellectual. Renunciation and self-restriction are considered repressive and dated concepts by this culture and by many of its gurus. However, the bottom-line message of Genesis 3 is that when humans exceed divine limits they harm themselves and manifest rebellion against God. People consumed with their own needs fracture the relationship with God and with fellow human beings (spouses, families, business associates). In sum: God blesses humanity by placing people in relationship (divine and human), which their own rebellion corrupts through distorted self-seeking.

SECOND LESSON: ROMANS 5:12–19

This reading takes up the theme of Adam's fall and counters it with the good news of new life in Christ. The Lutheran lectionary isolates vv. 12, 17–19 from the unit. Since the complicated reasoning and confusing sentence structure of the passage resists even careful study, it makes sense to construct just such a cohesive pericope for the purpose of public reading.

In vv. 1–11 Paul argues that God's justification and reconciliation through Jesus Christ are the basis of future salvation in which believers may rejoice. Now, in the remaining verses of chap. 5, Paul insists that as all people share in the consequences of Adam's disobedience, so all can share in the consequences of Christ's obedience. As death came to all because of sin, so life can come to all by God's act of grace.

The juxtaposition of Adam and Christ is a literary motif that holds this confusing portion of Romans together. While Adam is presented as a type *(typos)* of Christ, Paul's theological savvy leads him to contrast rather than compare the two. Adam and Christ are representative figures who responded differently in analogous circumstances. Exposed to temptation, the first Adam was disobedient and surrendered his true creaturehood; the second Adam was obedient unto death, even death on a cross, and is the progenitor of a new creation. One introduced into the world the rule of death, the other the rule of life.

The preacher will note that if read in the context of the entire letter, this passage will support neither a physical determinism nor a naive universalism. Paul does *not* say that human beings sin and die because they are physically descended from Adam. All God's creatures die because, like Adam, all sin (5:12; 3:23). Adam's story is our story. At the same time, Paul does *not* mean to say that the salvation of all is assured through the obedience of Christ. Elsewhere in Romans he insists that grace is received by faith (5:1), a gift of God that can be rejected.

The significance of the Adam/Christ contrast is crucial for Paul's theology (cf. 1 Cor. 15:21–22), and its interpretation is vital for the preacher. Does this text mean that all who (with Adam) choose sin are condemned to death, while all who (with Christ) are obedient receive the gift of life? If so, this is simply a Pauline version of the two ways, and in the sermon the listener can be challenged to a one-time decision to "choose life."

Or is Paul speaking here, not of two kinds of people (the sinners and the obedient), but of two perspectives on believing human beings? Insofar as humans are in rebellion against God, they are in Adam and subject to eternal death. Insofar as they are obedient to God, they are in Christ, justified and assured of eternal life. Most Pauline scholars believe the comparison is paradoxical rather than sequential. Believers are members of a race that has cut itself off from God (in Adam), but they have been clothed in a righteousness that is not their own (in Christ). Each believer is *simultaneously* a sinner who commits wicked actions (see Paul's distinction between "sin" and "transgression" in vv. 13–14) and a redeemed person who has received God's free gift of grace in Jesus Christ. If the old person/new person contrast is a paradox, then the preacher's task is to call listeners to *daily* repentance and renewal of life, *regularly* to renounce sin and trust in God's grace alone.

The preacher will note that the media tend to externalize and simplify the struggle between good and evil. The classic 1952 western *High Noon* is a study of one man facing danger and death alone. Film buffs will remember the plot. At 10:30 on the morning of his scheduled retirement, Will Kane, the United States marshal in Hadleyville, learns that a desperado named Frank Miller has just been released from the state prison. Five years earlier, the townspeople assisted the marshal when he arrested Miller, but now Miller and three fellow thugs are coming on the noon train. Their mission is a revenge killing of the veteran marshal, and the folks in Hadleyville no longer seem to care. When Kane seeks help, everyone finds some excuse to say no. So, with set face, Kane goes out to face death alone.

The imagination of Christians will turn to the Upper Room. With the meal over, and a hymn sung, a small group of friends moved into the night. Jesus' betrayal and arrest were at hand. The disciples fell asleep on watch. When a mob armed with swords and clubs descended upon the group, the disciples abandoned Jesus. "And they all forsook him, and fled" (Mark 14:50). Whether at high noon or in the dead of night, the stories seem similar. Abandoned, the hero goes alone to brave a horrible end. The preacher will have little trouble filling out a list of current folk heroes who are venerated for their courage in the face of death.

On the other hand, real life is rarely heroic. Seldom are there audiences to see temptations faced or flubbed. Daily suffering and private suffering grind people into the ground. The dialectical struggle between death and life, central to this text and to Paul's theology, is also an unpleasant fact of daily life.

Sam became depressed shortly after his retirement at age sixty-one. He began drinking more heavily, lacing his port wine with brandy (for his blood circulation, he said), starting to imbibe as early as 10:00 in the morning. This seemingly model Christian, president of the vestry, was a tense and guarded person, unable to share his feelings with others. Death and life contended in him, and his suicide shocked the entire congregation. Somehow, in his depression and despair, Sam was unable to trust in God's grace. Christ was giving him new life each day, but Sam felt alone. The preacher will have little trouble listing others like Sam, casualties in the ongoing and often private war between life and death. The struggle between life and death rages in persons like Sam who desperately need to hear the good news that they are acquitted and given life by the obedience of the second Adam.

GOSPEL: MATTHEW 4:1–11

A temptation account is traditional on the First Sunday in Lent. Jesus' forty days in the wilderness (together with the experiences of Israel, Moses, and Elijah) are the prototype for this period of preparation for Easter baptism.

Matthew's account of Jesus' temptation continues the twin themes of the baptismal narrative—the guidance and power of the Spirit and Jesus' obedience to the Father's will (3:13–17). The account of Jesus' struggle in the desert is followed by Matthew's account of the beginnings of the Galilean ministry (4:12–25).

The elaborate temptation narrative in Matthew is in stark contrast to the terse account in Mark 1:12–13. There are those who believe that the other Synoptics are elaborations of Mark. However, most commentators are convinced that another source (Q) lies behind the extended stories of Matthew and Luke (4:1–13).

Some scholars believe that Q, a collection of Jesus' sayings and deeds, was composed in the 60s, partly in opposition to the zealot dream of political power. The scenario spun out by these religious-political radicals had Israel overcoming the might of Rome. Aided by God's fantastic miracles, they had Jerusalem and its temple becoming the center of the world. Apparently the revolutionary zealots urged a program of violence and worldly power to achieve these ends, but the Q community rejected both as a temptation of Satan.[3] By the time Matthew was written, the fall of Jerusalem had put dreams of earthly power to rest. However, the narrative of Jesus trusting his life to God's direction in the face of temptation was retained because it highlighted the discipleship emphasis of the evangelist.

The Gospel of Luke agrees with Matthew in recording three acts of temptation, but Luke has the second and third temptations in reverse order. Various later manuscripts alter the order in Luke to match what they consider Matthew's original. Schweizer notes that Matthew's first two temptations begin similarly ("If you are the Son of God . . ."); "not until the third does Satan drop his disguise and demand to be worshiped."[4] Luke may have altered the order to climax his narrative in Jerusalem, foreshadowing Jesus' final triumph there (Luke 4:13).

While the twin themes of the guidance of the Spirit and Jesus' obedience to the Father link the baptismal and temptation stories, the new element in Matthew 4 is the devil, who attempts to deflect Jesus from his obedience to God. Historically, it is possible that Jesus faced special temptations at the outset of his ministry. Quite likely he was challenged again and again to prove his messiahship by performing miracles and was pressured to adjust his calling to the preconceptions of his contemporaries. However, the preacher should not treat this encounter in the desert as a one-time event. Even in Luke, where the devil seems to disappear until 22:3, there is no Satan-free period. Jesus contends repeatedly with illness and other challenges that were to the Hebraic mind manifestations of demonic power. Matthew 4 commences a lifelong battle of God's Son with temptation, although overcoming the evil one at the outset of his ministry does foreshadow Jesus' ultimate triumph in cross and resurrection.

The devil and demon possession remain issues for many today. Contemporary films of the supernatural employ the devil and his minions as stock characters. Films like *The Exorcist* are classic examples, in which Satan and his emissaries enter the lives of people who are otherwise normal. From time to time the media sensationalizes charges of demon possession and Satan worship. While the devil is *not* the central theme in this text, opportunities to correct superstitions about Satan should not be missed.

There is *no* absolute dualism in Scripture. All creatures are created by God, and their power is subordinate to the Creator's. In the Old Testament Satan ("accuser" or "adversary") is mentioned primarily in late writings, not as the incarnation of evil, but as an angel of the heavenly court whose duty is to accuse humans of wrongdoing (Job 1, 2; Zech. 3:1–2). Influenced by Persian sources, the idea of Satan developed in late apocryphal and rabbinical literature into the prince of evil, the chief opponent of God. It seems clear that Jesus accepted the reality of Satan and sometimes spoke about him in a poetic way (Luke 10:18). In the Bible and Christian theology the devil symbolizes a power greater than the sum total of human sin, a power that opposes God at every turn, but one that is ultimately defeated. A focus sentence may be helpful for preaching: The devil, a symbol of the power of evil, is an active but resistible enemy, already defeated by God in the ministry, cross, and resurrection of Jesus.

Despite the threefold nature of the temptation, it is exegetically and homiletically preferable to deal with the three scenes as diverse examples of Jesus' determination to obey God in the face of temptation. The use of quotations from Deuteronomy to counter the tempter's argument points to the central claim of God to total allegiance (Deut. 6:4–5). "According to Scripture, it is precisely those who are called by God that are tempted because they are torn between their God, who will not set them free, and the world, whose suffering they share."[5] This narrative was treasured in the church's oral tradition, in part because Jesus' resolve to obey God is a model for tempted Christians.

However, if Jesus is held up only as an example to emulate, listeners will derive little comfort from the sermon. Tempted humans, who sometimes succumb, are as much discouraged as aided by Jesus' sterling example. Jesus was human (like us), tempted as we are. At the same time he was God's Son (unlike us), able to resist the evil power, not captive to the spell. The really good news is that in his unique role as messiah, Jesus defeated the power of evil and the fruits of his victory are available to his followers. In the wilderness, Jesus, confessing his faith in God, overcame temptation on behalf of humanity, winning a victory that culminated in the final victory on the cross. In short: God empowers us by the Spirit to share in Jesus' victory; thereby God allows us to overcome (infinitely lesser) temptations of daily life and to remain faithful.

At the very beginning of the forty days of preparation for Easter baptism, the church used this narrative of Jesus' struggle to assist candidates in preparing for their own time of testing. From his baptism the path of Jesus led into the wilderness of temptation. At the same time, the experience of Jesus and the church is seen as antitypical of the experience of Israel's forty years in the wilderness. While it is the testimony of both Scripture and human experience that in the world believers encounter opposition to all that is of God, and that those most committed to being disciples will experience evil's temptation most acutely, it is also the experience of Christians that Jesus points the way to victory. The preacher desiring to emphasize the baptismal context can use this focus sentence: Baptized Christians, tempted to abandon their mission, are called to share the wilderness struggle and are enabled through the power of the Spirit to remain obedient to God.

For the preacher who may choose to focus on the bread temptation (4:3–4), the issue is *not* "manna in the wilderness" for hungry people, in spite of an apparent Old Testament allusion. Jesus is alone, and he is the hungry one. The conditional clause ("if you are the Son of God") underscores the essential nature of the temptation. Jesus is being enticed to use his power as Son of God for his own (rather than God's) ends, and he employs a quote from Deuteronomy (8:3) to repel the tempter. While our mission and powers differ radically from those of Jesus, we too are tempted to put our own bodily survival ahead of God's will. Under the title "The Fourth Temptation," one unidentified preacher focused on genuine human needs (like bread) that his contemporaries were putting ahead of God's will. Why not brainstorm with a group of lay persons about good things that corrupt?

Again, the scene set at the "pinnacle of the temple" (4:5–7) is not a temptation for Jesus to demonstrate power, since no audience is present for the miracle. However, the devil does entice Jesus to put God to the test (4:7). It is not necessary to go over Niagara Falls in a barrel or to drive more than one hundred miles per hour as a feat of prowess to put God to the test. Every day people violate precepts of physical and mental health as well as community standards of health and safety, counting on God to pull them through unscathed. Brainstorm and develop your own list.

The "very high mountain" scene (4:8–10) reveals the visionary nature of the temptation narrative—only metaphorically can one get high enough to "see it all." The devil offers the immediate power that would accrue to the ruler of all these kingdoms. The temptation to power is imaged starkly in films like *Wall Street* (business), *Patton* (military), and in the human interaction of Bull Meechum and his oldest son in The *Great Santini*. Popular autobiographies of figures in the world of business and industry project images of grasping for power and, if you read between the lines, of the weakness of power. In Matthew 4 Jesus represents the power of weakness that stands against the wiles of the devil.

The Second Sunday in Lent

Lutheran	Roman Catholic	Episcopal	Common Lectionary
Gen. 12:1–8	Gen. 12:1–4a	Gen. 12:1–8	Gen. 12:1–4a (4b–8)
Rom. 4:1–5, 13–17	2 Tim. 1:8b–10	Rom. 4:1–5, 13–17	Rom. 4:1–5 (6–12), 13–17
John 4:5–26	Matt. 17:1–9	John 3:1–17	John 3:1–17 *or* Matt. 17:1–9

On this Sunday we see God at work in history, calling Abraham to leave his country to found a nation that will become a blessing to the world.

Abraham's response to God's call makes him a model of faith, even for Christians, and contrasts with the tentative response to Jesus of the learned Nicodemus.

FIRST LESSON: GENESIS 12:1–4a (4b–8)

The call of Abram begins the second major section of the Book of Genesis. The primeval history of the Yahwistic (J) writer forms the bulk of the material in chapters 1–11. On the surface, this is the story of how human beings populated the earth; theologically, it is an account of human sin and the responsive judgment and preservation of God. From Adam and Eve to the tower of Babel we have the sad story of human rebellion which separated the Creator more and more from the creation. Yet with each punishment God found a way to preserve the people—until Genesis 11. At the end of the Babel narrative human unity lies fractured and the people scattered. However, God's judgment in Gen. 11:7–9 is the prelude to an extended history of salvation which begins with Abram.

Following the account of Babel, we find a genealogy constructed by the Priestly writer (P) (Gen. 11:10–27, 31, 32) that traces the line of descent from Shem, one of Noah's three sons, to Terah, the father of Nahor, Haran, and Abram. This list is a chronology of election that flows to a single person, Abram, the father of a new nation and the bearer of a promise of salvation for "all the families of the earth" (12:3).

Form critics label 12:1–3 a call narrative. In v. 1 God addresses Abram, commanding him to sever all his roots and trust himself to God's guidance. Verses 2–3 contain the actual promise of blessing. With vv. 4–8 an account of Abram's response begins.

A challenge for the preacher arises in the theological discontinuity between the Old Testament and New Testament understanding of "blessing." In both testaments God is the giver of blessings. However, in Semitic thought "blessing" is concrete and is measured in material things like descendants (Gen. 13:16), fame (12:2), land (12:7), crops, and herds. In the New Testament blessing is "spiritualized" (cf. the Beatitudes, Matt. 5:2–12) and can be returned as thanks to God (2 Cor. 1:3).

At the start of an exclusive covenant relationship with a single human being we have the promise of an inclusive salvation to encompass the nations of the world. What some commentators label "primeval history" (Genesis 1–11) is actually an intimation of the universal conclusion to the drama of salvation. This prehistory foreshadows the end in the beginning.

The pattern of vision exhibited in these early chapters of Genesis, from wide angle (chaps. 1–11), to narrow (12:1—2a, b), to wide (12:2c–3), is instructive. From time to time most of us get lost in life's particularities. We lose a sense of the total picture. Show people a snapshot in which they appear and the eye searches for the self first. Only after finding themselves will the majority of individuals take note of others in the photograph and the location of the shot. Texts such as this one enable us to find our place in the picture of God's dealing with the human race. Gaining a perspective, seeing where we fit as individuals and congregations in God's plan for the world, assists believers to find meaning in the seeming randomness of everyday.

This loss of perspective is a common motif in novels and films of persons in combat all the way from *A Walk in the Sun* to *Platoon*. Repeatedly, the common infantryman is ordered to take and hold objectives that seem worthless. Why fight and die for a particular farmhouse or ridge, only to pull back from the position as quickly as it has been secured? The dilemma of not being able to see "the big picture" is repeated daily as the individual engineer in a large corporation, the foreman of a construction crew, or the individual congregation in a diocese or district struggles to find meaning in assignments that seem confused or inadvisable.

The story of Abram is intended to reassure believers that despite all blunders and confusion God has a comprehensive vision. Whether or not the author has written the final chapter, the broad contours of the plot are known. To summarize: The God who called Abraham to leave his country for a land to be his by promise, includes us (where we are, with the talents and challenges given to us) in divine activity in history to bring a divine blessing to the world.

At the same time, Christians will read Abram's story from a New Testament perspective, which suggests an overlay. God chooses Abram to be the father of a nation. God chooses Jesus Christ to become the parent of a new people, the church.

This plot line raises what has been called the "scandal of particularity." Why Abram? "How odd of God to choose the Jews." "Can any good thing come out of Nazareth?" (John 1:46). Why the church? Try this focus sentence for preaching: Following the pattern of the choice of Abram and Jesus of Nazareth God continues to call unlikely persons and congregations to be a blessing to others.

At the beginning of this call narrative Abram is commanded to leave everything behind (land, home, and clan), to uproot his family, and to trust himself to the direction of God (12:1). In a mobile society like ours it may be useful to engage listeners at a natural point of interest for them; namely, the separation anxiety of uprooting a family to move to a new community. People may enjoy a transcultural retelling of the biblical story that adds packing boxes, moving vans, and checking out the local school system to the Genesis narrative. The psychological dynamics that accompany moving are similar to those of any loss; they include anger, guilt, depression, and loneliness. However, the preacher will assist listeners to move to a deeper understanding of loss; that is, separation from prior commitments and life-styles in order to serve God faithfully. The story highlights the obedience of Abram, Sarai, and Lot in response to God's promise. It makes Abram a model of faith for New Testament writers (see Heb. 11:8–10 as well as today's second reading, from Romans 4). Similarly, believers are called to be Christian, called to respond in faith to the will of God for their lives.

In the book *Future Shock,* Alvin Toffler discussed "personal stability zones" that contemporary nomads build into their lives.[6] To compensate for the rapid change to which they are subjected some people restore dated automobiles, wear clothing styles of earlier eras, or hold rigidly to dated routines. When transcience and turnover leave most things up for grabs, to what do people cling? At the deepest level what we cling to is our "god." The theological message can be summarized for preaching: When called to leave the security of the known for the unknown, like Abram and Sarai we are able to obey by clinging to the promises of God and by experiencing God's presence in worship even in a "strange land."

The reaction of listeners to a text such as this suggests a possible way to structure the message using what rhetoricians term a "ladder." The preacher will plan the sermon to engage people where they are in order to assist them to move (in two or three steps) from an area of common understanding to a more profound engagement with the message of the text.

It should be noted that in studying call narratives lay persons commonly ask how the people of the Bible knew it was God who spoke to them. They are really asking how God speaks today and how they are to know the divine will for their lives. While this text does not address the issue directly, it is clear that Abram and Sarai were persons of worship and prayer (12:7–8, and the focus sentence above). Abram did not know where he was going, but he did know who was going along. Total clarity about the will of God is seldom possible in advance, but faith nurtured in worship responds in obedience.

The leader of worship will observe that Abram and Sarai's renaming by God does not occur until Genesis 17. However, it will lessen listener confusion to explain why the second reading uses the name Abraham. Most preachers will employ the more familiar *Abraham* and *Sarah* in the sermon.

SECOND LESSON: ROMANS 4:1–5 (6–12), 13–17

This reading from Romans 4 contributes to the thematic unity of the Sunday by focusing on Abraham's trust in the divine promise. Having introduced the central theme of righteousness through faith immediately prior to our lesson (3:21–31), Paul uses this portion of his letter to the church at Rome to support that affirmation with scriptural evidence. By making Abraham the prototype of Christian faith, the apostle contrasts his understanding of the way righteousness is appropriated with a legalistic view.

In Rom. 4:1–5 Paul asserts that Abraham cannot boast before God, since he did not earn righteousness but had it reckoned to him as a gift of grace. Verses 6–8 employ scriptural references to support the thesis that God justifies the ungodly. In vv. 9–12 Paul makes clear that by taking Abraham's path to righteousness, the fence of the law is circumvented for both believing Jews and Gentiles. The final unit in this reading, vv. 13–17, reinforces the theme that God's relationship with Abraham and with those who share the faith of Abraham is based on a promise, the correlates of which are grace and faith. In v. 17 the apostle forges an insightful link between justification and resurrection. Justification anticipates the resurrection of the dead in the sense that it gives life to those who because of sin deserve only death.

This passage is simultaneously a treasure trove and a mine field for the preacher-theologian who desires to raise a congregation's level of understanding of its doctrinal heritage. The list of theological terms to be clarified as part of the *exegetical* work of sermon preparation is lengthy. It includes, but is not limited to, words like flesh, reckon, justify, works, righteousness, blessing, circumcision, faith, seal, promise, wrath, and grace. Lively metaphors once, these words have become technical terms in theological dictionaries. Words like faith and grace ought to be part of the vocabulary of laity, but many other terms are better translated into contemporary idiom.

Words of warning are in order here, for sermons that focus on key theological terms can be disastrous. It is usually a mistake to allow the exegetical process to affect the sequence of the sermon. In the study, discerning the first-century meaning of a word like "righteousness" is an early step in the exegetical process, but leading with that in the pulpit is likely to kill listener interest. Perhaps the account of an ongoing trial or grand jury investigation will be a way to connect with the sense of righteousness as justice or making things right again. Beginning the sermon with relationships strained and broken in the "horizontal" (person-to-person) dimension of life may establish an image for understanding the good news of the "vertical" relationship restored at God's initiative.

In this reading Paul addresses the question of *how* a person is justified. Central to Rom. 4:1–5 is a contrast between righteousness as wages for work, as a person's due, and righteousness through faith as graceful gift of God. Axioms like "a day's work for a day's pay" suggest that both labor and management understand the correlatives "work" and "due." The good news of the text is that Abraham's faith "is reckoned as righteousness" (v. 5). To focus: Those who misunderstand a right relationship with God as wages due for good works are reminded by Paul through the example of Abraham that God restores sinners to a right relationship by grace through faith.

Striving to be true to the form and spirit as well as to the message of Romans 4 could result in a sermon that presents the thesis that Abraham is a prototype of Christian faith and supports that thesis by citing and interpreting scriptural evidence. The preacher needs to ask whether this thesis is really a matter of debate today and whether rational argument is the most effective way to reach contemporary listeners. "Most people, even educated people, do not listen analytically but are affected by the pattern of imagery in an utterance."[7] The mind commonly works by association rather than by logical movement from point to point. The imagination leaps from image to image.

Abraham, who went forth from Haran trusting in the promise of God (Gen. 12:1–4), is the prototype of Christians who respond to God's call even when the path ahead is hidden. Linking Paul's analysis in vv. 13–17 to the narrative in Genesis 12 may assist listeners to visualize Abraham's risky venture. Church history and contemporary experience are full of stories of believers who staked their lives on God's grace. Finally, the preacher can link biblical, historical, and contemporary models of faith to each Christian's baptismal call to trust and obey. To focus: In baptism, God calls believers like Abraham, _____, and _____ to trust each day in the divine promise of life.

GOSPEL: JOHN 3:1–17

In this reading Jesus teaches Nicodemus that new life is a gift from above and not a human achievement. This life comes as the wind (3:8), free of human direction and control.

Nicodemus, who came to Jesus by night and who assisted in the Lord's burial (19:39), is mentioned only in the Fourth Gospel. There he represents a cadre of Jewish leaders who were attracted to Jesus on the basis of his signs, but who remained secret followers for fear of being expelled from the synagogue (12:42). For the Johannine community, excommunicated by their fellow Jews for following Jesus openly, a secret faith like that of Nicodemus was inadequate.

The Sanhedrin, the highest governing body of the Jewish people, was composed of seventy priests and laity with members belonging to the two major religious parties, Sadducees and Pharisees. The high priest presided over this council. Nicodemus was both a member of the Sanhedrin and a Pharisee.

Elsewhere in John officials who become enemies of the gospel are labeled simply "the Jews." To avoid the Johannine slur with its connotation of racial/religious bias, preachers can accurately refer to persons like Nicodemus as "religious and political leaders" or simply "the religious establishment."

In the structure of the book the story of Nicodemus follows accounts of the faith of the disciples at Cana (2:1–11) and the unbelief of the Jews, which resulted in the temple cleansing (2:13–22). Following these polar examples of faith and unbelief, and after the statement that many in Jerusalem believed because of his signs (2:23–25), the Nicodemus story is a mediating example of partial faith.

The Nicodemus scene is a Johannine discourse. Raymond Brown has noted that three interrogatives (one implicit) of Nicodemus (vv. 2, 4, 9) evoke responses of Jesus beginning with "I solemnly assure you" (vv. 3, 5, 11).[8] The narrative portion of the discourse ends when references to Nicodemus end (v. 9), but theological reflection continues. In John it is seldom clear where Jesus' words and those of the evangelist begin and end.

John appears to use gnostic imagery (the redeemer myth) to proclaim a message of new life. Life does not come by physical descent or by special knowledge *(gnosis)* but by means of a redeemer from heaven. Verses 2–8 focus on birth from above through the Spirit, and vv. 9–21 assert that this rebirth is possible only when the Son has ascended to the Father.

The detail that Nicodemus came to Jesus "by night" (v. 2) appears insignificant at first. In the context of Jesus' own ministry it may be that the Pharisee came "by night" because he was concerned about what his colleagues might think, or the detail may simply reflect the pattern of academic discourse late into the night. However, for the evangelist darkness and night symbolize the realm of evil and ignorance (cf. 9:4 and 11:10).

Likewise, in the mythic, surreal Vietnam of *Apocalypse Now* (1979) the journey upriver is symbolized by an increasing darkness in both lighting and human behavior. The closer Martin Sheen's gunboat and its crew come to the renegade Colonel Kurtz, the more sinister and senseless the violence becomes. Francis Coppola borrowed the film's journey motif from Joseph Conrad's novel *Heart of Darkness*. Coppola made Conrad's journey up the Congo a metaphor for a journey upriver into the darkness and insanity of the Vietnam War. Martin Sheen, commander of the gunboat, tainted by the darkness himself, presses on to reveal the insanity that waits at the end of the river.

At the same time, for the evangelist, light signifies revelation through Jesus Christ. The conclusion to this unit (vv. 19–21, not part of the Gospel reading) summarizes the claim that in Jesus the light comes into a dark world and is rejected by many, while those who come to the light (like Nicodemus) can be saved. A light turned on in a seldom-used basement or attic exposes what is hidden in darkness. For the evangelist the coming of the light is both judgment (vv. 19, 20) and grace (v. 21). The Johannine dichotomy of nonbelievers and believers, those who prefer darkness and those who come to the light, is overdrawn. Nevertheless, the real emphasis in this passage and elsewhere in the Fourth Gospel is the Revealer who brings the good news of rebirth.

The question of Jesus' identity is a central focus of John 3. Nicodemus, drawn by Jesus' signs, calls him "a teacher come from God" (v. 2). Like Sheen, Jesus has a wisdom that sees deeply into life's darkness. Later in the discourse, it becomes clear that Jesus is more than an insightful human; his is also the true light from heaven. Jesus knows the truth because he has come from above (v. 13). Jesus is God's "only Son" sent by a loving Father to save a perishing world (3:16–17).

The double meaning of the Greek *anōthen*, both "again" and "from above," is crucial in the discourse. This wordplay is employed by the evangelist as a technique to advance the reader's understanding of the new birth (v. 3). Nicodemus protests the physiological impossibility of being born twice (v. 4), but in response Jesus expands his statement to focus on birth from above, from the Spirit (v. 5). Again in v. 8 the writer cleverly plays on the double meaning of "wind" and "spirit" (Greek *pneuma* as well as the Hebrew *ruah)*. The point of the entire section is that humans take on flesh when they enter the world, but the heavenly kingdom is entered only when humans are begotten again by God's Spirit. In summary: To those who, like Nicodemus, are drawn from darkness to Jesus the light, God offers the gift of rebirth in (water and) the Spirit and a challenge to journey in the light.

In the Fourth Gospel, children of flesh become God's children when the resurrected Jesus gives the Spirit. Because baptism is not mentioned by name in John 3, a few commentators question whether the evangelist associated the gift of the Spirit with washing in water. The text does speak of being born "of water and the Spirit" (v. 5). Since this story is preceded and followed by references to the baptismal ministries of *both* John and Jesus (1:33; 4:1–2), the context suggests that baptism is intended in v. 5 (cf. also Eph. 5:26). A sermon based on John 3 can reinforce the connection between baptism and the Spirit.

John 3:14–15 is a self-contained analogy of Christ's redemptive act to the brazen serpent incident in Num. 21:4–9. The preacher may wish to defer attention to this brief unit until it is paired with Numbers 21 in year B of the lectionary.

In the Numbers account, the people who had forgotten the covenant are saved, not by the physical action of looking at the *saraf* (snake image), but by the God of whom they are reminded. God both convicts the people and provides a means of healing. For the evangelist the comparison is not to the serpent but to the "lifting up." In John, lifting up has the double meaning of death on the cross and exaltation to the presence of God. Being lifted up on the cross is (to eyes of faith) the victory that the Synoptics proclaim in connection with resurrection appearances and empty tomb stories (cf. 12:32). To focus for preaching: Just as God used the uplifted serpent to preserve life, so that uplifted (crucified) Son of man is God's means to draw rebels to receive the gift of eternal life.

In our lives we lift up many different "objects" to see and follow. Flags of various sorts are raised to proclaim allegiance to governments. Salutes are raised to military figures and rulers. Students hold diplomas aloft. Sports fans raise a single finger to proclaim themselves "number one." Banners of protest are displayed for or against one cause or another. It was Luther's insight that the things we elevate and venerate become our gods.

In this passage (v. 11) we are called to lift up Christ, to witness to the Son that God has lifted up for us. Believers are challenged to testify that God is the source of new life mediated by Jesus Christ. This juxtaposition is insightful: In the face of what we today lift up to see and follow, God lifts up the Son of man for our hope and salvation and empowers us to testify to that gift.

The Third Sunday in Lent

Lutheran	Roman Catholic	Episcopal	Common Lectionary
Isa. 42:14–21	Exod. 17:3–7	Exod. 17:1–7	Exod. 17:3–7
Eph. 5:8–14	Rom. 5:1–2, 5–8	Rom. 5:1–11	Rom. 5:1–11
John 9:1–41	John 4:5–42	John 4:5–26, 39–42	John 4:5–26 (27–42)

God, who at Meribath gave wandering Hebrews water to quench human thirst (Exod. 17:3–7), at a well in Samaria promised "living water" to quench life's deepest thirst (John 4:5–26). Today's theological message is that God fills the profound needs of humanity.

FIRST LESSON: ISAIAH 42:14–21 (OPTION 1)

Only the Lutheran lectionary appoints Isaiah 42 as today's first lesson. The story of God's activity on behalf of spiritually blind exiles is an obvious companion reading for John 9:1–41, Jesus' healing of a man born blind. A discussion of John 9 is found beginning on page 46.

The immediate context of this reading employs the image of blindness in a way that ties the entire chapter together. However, most commentators suggest that vv. 14–17 and 18–25 are independent oracles that can be treated separately for preaching purposes. This study focuses on the first oracle.

Deutero-Isaiah was a prophet of the exile whose prophetic activity occurred in the latter days of the Babylonian Empire. Scholars mention 550

B.C., the rise of Cyrus, as a likely benchmark for the beginning of this nameless prophet's ministry.

Claus Westermann considers 42:14–17 a "proclamation of salvation."[9] Typical of the form, God admits restraint in the face of the people's suffering ("for a long time," v. 14a), but now God indicates a changed attitude in response to their lament (v. 14b). The Lord intends to intervene in history on behalf of the exiles (vv. 15–16). Yahweh's own people will be led through the desert to their homeland, while those who trusted in idols will be "put to shame" (v. 17).

In the eyes of many the fall of Jerusalem, the destruction of the temple, and the end of the Davidic line meant the end of Yahweh's activity on behalf of the people. Far from home, far from their own land, many believers felt separated from God and abandoned. The gods of Babylon appeared victorious and some Israelites worshiped them. Many who remained faithful accused Yahweh of forsaking the chosen people. But those who made this charge were blind to the meaning of the exile, blind to their own unfaithfulness, and blind to the viability of God (42:18–21).

Spiritual blindness is a symptom common to those who have suffered personal or corporate reversals. Blindness is experienced in congregations when attendance drops dramatically, when commitment to the program wanes, when loss of membership is pronounced, when key leaders die, or when a pastor leaves to accept another call. One dimension of the grief that follows any loss is an inability to perceive clearly. Sadness and despair cause mourners to become myopic. Judgment is affected adversely.

But Deutero-Isaiah's good news is that God has not abandoned the people. God is about to do a new thing. As in the exodus from Egypt, God will lead blind people safely across a desert, transformed in poetic imagination into a garden. The message of hope for contemporary listeners is that this same God is at work today. To focus for preaching: The God who used Cyrus, a gentile conqueror, to free exiles from a Babylonian prison is at work today, in ways we often do not discern, to lead us who feel forsaken in the way we ought to go.

One intention of oracles that proclaim salvation is to evoke hope among the hopeless. Second Isaiah's language of praise and poetic rapture was intended to assist listeners to recapture the image of God as one powerful enough to effect deliverance. The prophet employed language intended to arouse people whose lamp of faith was dim or extinguished. To be faithful to the text and to evoke similar hope, the preacher should employ language and a style of delivery designed to encourage and motivate listeners.

The structure of the proclamation of salvation lends itself to sermon design. The hopelessness of the people and their cry for assistance is acknowledged at the outset. This is developed both in contemporary terms and with reference to the situation of exiles. In the developing plot line the good news of God's attitude and intervention follow, with the consequences spelled out in terms of judgment (v. 17) and grace (vv. 15–16) for blind persons then and now.

FIRST LESSON: EXODUS 17:3–7 (OPTION 2)

Most lectionaries appoint as the first reading for today the story of how Moses quenched Israel's thirst with water from the rock (Exod. 17:3–7). This experience is part of the so–called wilderness tradition (15:22—18:27), located between the story of the miraculous rescue at the sea and the arrival of the people at Sinai (9:1). These tribal memories of nomadic life in the desert have been arranged by the Priestly writer (P) into a fairly coherent story undergirded by P's theology of a divine plan of God for the people. While P compiled and edited the wilderness material either late in the exile or following it, the Yahwist (J) source for this story is from the reign of David or Solomon.

Exodus 17:3–7 is a narrative that seems to have a history of oral transmission from the time when the Hebrews lived a seminomadic existence. As herdsmen they were dependent upon oases where pure water could be found in quantity for people and animals. Later, this saga seems to have become an etiology—a story explaining the origin of a name, place, or cultic practice. In this later version of the tale the primary focus is on the meaning of Meribah (contention), with a later hand having added references to Massah (vv. 2, 7) with the catchword "put to the proof" *(nissah)*.

It was a firm tenet of Israel's theology that God proved and guided the people in the wilderness, preparing them for later entry into the promised land. The motif of privation, particularly a lack of food and water, recurs in the materials. The theme of a lack of water is introduced at the very beginning of the wilderness account (15:22–25).

Exodus 17:3–7 (see Num. 20:2–13) is an example of the so-called murmuring motif that occurs first in Exod. 15:22–25. The people direct their murmuring to Moses the leader and to God who gives the marching orders. Through Moses the complaint of the people is heard, and Yahweh responds graciously (cf. also 16:2–21).

The narrative begins in v. 3 with the people arriving at a place in the desert where they did not find water. Their complaining is directed to

Moses and to Yahweh. When Moses cries to God for help, he is directed to choose several elders as witnesses and to strike a particular rock (on which God is said to stand) with the rod used earlier to strike the Nile (7:17, 20). Immediately, water gushes forth, and Moses names the spring Meribah, "place of faultfinding."

Since God is not *visibly* at the head of the church and since it remains the tendency of sinful humans to distrust God's leadership and guidance, this ancient story has contemporary claim. Theologically, the story is an example of the paradigm of sin and grace. The people rebel against God's direction even as God remains faithful to the promise. In this broad sense it is the story of God's people in every age as they struggle to remain faithful in the midst of human need. In summary: God meets the needs of the people as they are led from promise to fulfillment.

The tendency to find fault and to oppose leadership is one way that sin continues to manifest itself in the lives of those being redeemed. The preacher would do well to research the psychological dynamic of "resistance" as a way to confront and deal with this phenomenon. We may summarize the motif of murmuring in Exod. 17:3–7 thus: God directs the people, in spite of their complaining and even against their wills, using leaders able to listen to their faultfinding, toward the fulfillment of God's purpose.

SECOND LESSON: ROMANS 5:1–11

The second lesson of the Lutheran lectionary, Eph. 5:8–14, is discussed under the Fourth Sunday in Lent, page 44, where it is appointed for reading in most other lectionaries.

Having focused on the heart of what he called "my gospel" in chaps. 3 and 4, Paul in chap. 5 goes on to discuss several consequences of justification by faith.

Paul suggests that peace with God is a present gift of grace and that believers look forward in hope of sharing the glory of God (vv. 1–2). Moreover, because of the love of God poured out through the Holy Spirit, believers are able to rejoice in their afflictions (vv. 3–5). They are sustained by that love of God for sinners exhibited in Jesus Christ (vv. 6–8), whose death reconciles them to God and assures them of salvation at the end (vv. 9–11).

While justification and reconciliation are metaphors pointing backward to what was accomplished by God through the death of Jesus, both simultaneously also point forward to the moment when God's promises will be fully realized. This paradox of *already* justified/reconciled but *not yet* saved is typical of Paul's conviction that believers stand between two decisive moments in the work of redemption. With Jesus the last age has been inaugurated but is not yet consummated. Should the preacher decide to explore this paradox, in which both "terms" are true, most likely the sermon design would have two main sections or movements.

Contemporary listeners influenced by positive thinking and feel-good therapists are apt to substitute "peace of mind" when they hear the word "peace" in v. 1. This stressed generation has been conditioned by pop psychology to think of peace as a mindset that occurs when emotions are free of tension and conflict. A trip to the psychology section of a local bookstore will reveal a surprising number of selections with "peace" as part of the title.

However, Rom. 5:1 speaks of "peace with God" as the condition effected by the death of Jesus in which the bonds between God and God's people are restored. When estrangement ends and a new relationship with God begins, the Bible calls the state "peace." Thus, peace and reconciliation are different metaphors for the same reality. Generally the Greek word for peace *(eirēnē)* picks up the positive nuances of the Hebrew word *(shalom)*— harmony, wholeness, and completeness. In biblical usage, peace is a condition of the last days that is experienced already by those in Christ. To focus for sermon preparation: In human relationships, when estrangement is overcome and reconciliation is effected, believers experience the peace-making of the risen Christ as a foretaste of the peace to come.

Paul's declaration of joy in suffering will be offensive to some (vv. 2b–5), yet the apostle does not urge suffering for its own sake. That is masochism. Suffering as such is not beneficial. What may be beneficial is suffering that, like the suffering of the Hebrews in the wilderness, leads to life. God entered into human experience in the suffering of Israel and of Jesus Christ to give life to a suffering world. Those who suffer with Christ, that is, for the cause for which Christ suffered, participate with the risen Lord in the ongoing work of reconciliation. Most people regard either a lack of suffering or an escape from suffering as a mark of divine favor. However, in Paul's theology of the cross the suffering of Christ—and of Christ's own—is an expected part of life.

> The object . . . is to identify oneself with the suffering that is already there in one's world, to let oneself be led by the love of Christ into solidarity with those who suffer, and to accept the consequences of this solidarity in the

belief—the joyful belief—that in this way God is still at work in the world, making a conquest of its sin and suffering from within.[10]

To focus for preaching: Christians, who suffer with Christ as partners in the work of reconciliation, may rejoice because their sufferings point toward the sure and certain hope of Christ's final conquest of sin and suffering.

GOSPEL: JOHN 4:5–26 (27–42)

Most lectionaries conclude this pericope with v. 26. However, because the evangelism emphasis in vv. 27–42 is a natural extension of the narrative, worship planners may choose to lengthen the public reading.

Persons who read John 4 as a historical report are confronted with numerous difficulties. Why did it take all the disciples to do the marketing, leaving an exhausted Jesus to request a drink from a Samaritan woman? Why was Jesus' party without the essential leather bucket and rope that travelers would need to draw water from wells along the way? Why did the woman come to the well alone in the heat of the day? How did Jesus know of the woman's previous marriages and her present living arrangement?

Other scholars seek to reconstruct an original nucleus or source document about an encounter between Jesus and a woman (possibly a Samaritan). After asking her for a drink and engaging her in conversation Jesus makes a pronouncement about the imminence of the kingdom of God. The point of the story has been clouded or lost in the narrative of the fourth evangelist who expanded the original tale to cover many items of interest in his own church as a result of the Samaritan mission.

Ernst Haenchen posits a source narrative that "presents Jesus more or less as a miracle worker."[11] Haenchen argues that the fourth evangelist corrects the theology of his source by inserting his own material into the text (particularly vv. 19–27). If the text is read without the verses named, the preacher experiences a reasonably coherent narrative which *may* be a close approximation of the evangelist's source. In the Fourth Gospel Jesus brings the final revelation of God, proclaims salvation, exposes sin, and inaugurates the true worship of God.

In the literary context of the Fourth Gospel the author uses transitional verses (4:1–3) to move Jesus from Jerusalem (2:12—3:21) and Judea (3:22–36) to Samaria (4:4–42).

A bit of history is essential to understand the contention between Jews and Samaritans and their worship traditions evidenced in this text. When

Shalmaneser, the king of Assyria, conquered Samaria in 722 B.C. he deported many of the native people and brought other conquered populations to be settled there (2 Kings 17). In Jesus' day it was charged that these colonists intermarried with persons left behind, corrupted the race, and developed a heathen cult. After the Babylonian exile, when Samaritans obstructed the efforts of Ezra and Nehemiah to rebuild Jerusalem and reestablish the temple of Yahweh (Ezra 4:2; Neh. 2:19), the strained relationship between Jews and Samaritans deteriorated into a heated rivalry.

Both preacher and listeners may be struck initially by the image of water prominent in vv. 6–15. In the Middle East, as elsewhere in the world, the presence or absence of water determined where settlements grew up and whether people and animals lived or died. Villages were often constructed around wells, and wells became a gathering place for women who came regularly to draw water. Wells were shafts into the ground lined with stone. The top of the well was usually surrounded by a wall of stone capped with a lid to protect the well against dirt and refuse. Persons who came to draw water brought along their own leather pails and ropes. While a clay jar might have been carried on a woman's shoulder or head to transport water home, a rope and pail were essential to draw the water that filled the jar.[12]

The confusion and misunderstanding evident in all the Johannine signs is apparent here as well. The woman mistakes Jesus' challenge to ask him for "living water" for an offer to provide water from the clear spring at the bottom of the well. For the narrator this exchange is an opportunity to introduce Jesus' discussion of the water that quenches spiritual thirst, water "welling up to eternal life" (v. 14). The water that gives spiritual satisfaction, the water essential to eternal life, is a gift of Jesus.

Some scholars believe the evangelist understands living water as Jesus' revelation and teaching. The background of this interpretation is the scribal identification of Wisdom with Torah. In John's account Jesus is depicted as the true Wisdom that replaces the law. The woman seems to acknowledge Jesus' claim by calling him a "prophet" (v. 19).

Other commentators argue that living water is the Spirit communicated by Jesus. This seems plausible, since elsewhere in John it is the Spirit who gives life (6:63). Later in this very dialogue the theme of the Spirit is introduced overtly (4:23–24). However, there may be no need to choose between the two since in Johannine thought symbols are rich and suggestive of various meanings.

In the Johannine community this text would have been read in light of that church's own experience of baptism, an event in which natural water became a sign of new life in Christ. When Lent evolved in the church as a season to prepare converts for Easter initiation, this text's baptismal overtones caused it to be read in worship. Despite the fact that baptism is never mentioned by name in the reading, the preacher should not neglect the association. Try working with this theological message: To people who thirst for something to assuage their deepest yearnings, the risen Christ comes in water and Spirit offering the gift of eternal life.

Surely, one implication of the dialogue between Jesus and a Samaritan woman would be to underscore Jesus' conflict with the entire scribal casuistry in which some persons (by reason of gender, race, or religion) are unclean. Jesus' proclivity for responding as a human being to other human beings and for reaching out in concrete situations to the sick and outcast persons of his day broke ritualistic barriers between clean and unclean. In the kingdom of God, as preached by Jesus, distinctions dissolve, and all who respond are "blessed." Paul names baptism into Christ as the point where barriers of race, sex, and station are overcome (Gal. 3:27–29).

In this lection one barrier surmounted by Jesus is that of gender.[13] When the disciples returned from shopping "they marveled that he was talking with a woman" (v. 27). Public conversation by a pious rabbi with a woman was unthinkable. "One does not speak with a woman on the street, not even his own wife, and certainly not with another woman, on account of gossip."[14]

If Jesus had been concerned about gossip, then the woman's life-style and reputation would have been added reason for him to keep his distance. In the "miracle tradition" of the evangelist's source Jesus had magical knowledge of the woman, her five previous husbands, and her live-in male companion. Despite this, he did not hesitate to initiate conversation with her.

The preacher will recognize in this story of a Jewish rabbi sitting in quiet conversation with a woman, sharing stories, and reaching out to her as a human being, a fine image of inclusion. In a culture rife with unconventional life-styles and sexual relationships, when Christians are tempted primarily to condemn its sinful ways, members of the church need to be reminded that Christ died for *all*. To summarize: Followers of the Lord, who shattered conventions in daring to converse with a woman of questionable morals, are challenged to relate to all members of society while sharing the good news of community in Christ.

Likewise, barriers of race and religion are overcome in the meeting of the Jewish rabbi and the Samaritan woman. Samaria, populated by persons of mixed race and hybrid religion, was "across the tracks" for Jews. The statement that Jesus "had to pass through Samaria" (v. 4) should not be pressed. Travelers routinely went around Samaria by way of the Jordan valley to avoid passing through this despised place. Avoiding persecution at the hands of the Pharisees is hinted at (v. 1) as one reason why Jesus took the "throughway" rather than the river route around the land of half-breeds and heretics. A few scholars read the "had to" of v. 4 as compliance with the will of God.

Most listeners will understand the image "the other side of the tracks" whether or not they have experienced a place where a railroad actually bisects the community. "Across the tracks" suggests distinctive smells and dress, substandard housing, particular vocal inflections, or different skin color. "Ghetto" may be too strong a term, but the expression "the other side of the tracks" is reserved for places and people who are different.

The "other side of the tracks" also signifies a state of mind. Watch little children play together in a city nursery school and observe that differences go unnoticed at the doll house or box of blocks. At the same time, adults do notice, feel, and respond to differences. Axioms grow up and are passed from parents to children. "Never go alone." "Don't go after dark." "Never marry one." People from across the tracks evoke fear and prejudice. To focus: Jesus both directs and motivates followers to reach out to those across the tracks who have experienced isolation and rejection.

The love of Christ motivates all reaching out. However, the preacher will stress the need for Christians to move beyond one-to-one helpfulness. Love ought to seek justice for excluded persons, even as it seeks to eliminate the conditions that lead to their rejection.

The rivalry between Samaritans and Jews reached its culmination in the erection of a rival temple on Mount Gerizim, which had been destroyed by the time of Jesus. Each tradition sought to limit correct worship to its particular place and to identify its own form of worship as normative. Contemporary believers also seek to make shrines of their places of worship, stained-glass windows, and family pews. But just as the dawning of the eschaton spelled the end of Jewish cultic practices for John's church, so the gift of the Spirit frees contemporary Christians from bondage to particular buildings, appointments, worship books, and liturgies as the community of the risen Lord seeks to worship "in spirit and in truth."

The Fourth Sunday in Lent

Lutheran	Roman Catholic	Episcopal	Common Lectionary
Hos. 5:15—6:2	1 Sam. 16:1b, 6–7, 10–13a	1 Sam. 16:1–13	1 Sam. 16:1–13
Rom. 8:1–10	Eph. 5:8–14	Eph. 5:8–14	Eph. 5:8–14
Matt. 20:17–28	John 9:1–41	John 9:1–13, 28–38	John 9:1–41

Themes of light and darkness connect the second and third readings and make them mutually reinforcing if preached together. The light that Christ gives to the blind man in John 9 has its counterpart in the way of life commended to believers in Ephesians 5. The first reading stresses the seriousness with which God views human obedience.

FIRST LESSON: 1 SAMUEL 16:1–13

The two Books of Samuel are a single book in the Hebrew Scriptures. The portion we refer to as 1 Samuel focuses on three principal characters: Samuel, Saul, and David. All three are significant for an understanding of the reading appointed for the Fourth Sunday in Lent.

The story of how God used the prophet Samuel to reject King Saul immediately precedes this lesson (1 Samuel 15). Although Saul had won a mighty victory over the Amalekites, his unwillingness to follow God's marching orders to destroy all Amalekites and their possessions made him unfit to hold his position. Thus, according to a later source of 1 Samuel, the word of the Lord came to Samuel, "I repent that I have made Saul king; for he has turned back from following me, and has not performed my commandments" (15:10–11). According to this strand of tradition, rebellion and stubbornness in failing to heed the word of God disqualified Saul, and Samuel was dispatched to notify him that God's support for his kingship had ended. In the arrangement of the book this encounter between Samuel and Saul foreshadows God's selection of a new ruler.

First Samuel 16:1–13, the appointed reading, focuses on Samuel's journey to Bethlehem to appoint David as the king of Israel. The rest of the chapter (16:14–23) explains how David won a position at the court of Saul and rose to replace the one whose armor he bore as leader of the nation.

At least two sources have been combined in this portion of Samuel. The clue is that the court musician, who soothes the king's depression and becomes his "favorite" in chap. 16, appears as a strange shepherd lad to slay Goliath in chap. 17 (see esp. vv. 55–58). However, this discrepancy does not affect the interpretation of the pericope.

Although the Old Testament contains memories of the anointing of both priests (Exod. 29:7) and prophets (1 Kings 19:16), the primary association of this ceremony is the selection of kings. So definite is the association of this ritual with kingship that rulers came to be called "the Lord's anointed" (16:6). Apparently, olive oil was used for the solemn rite. Animal sacrifice and ritual washing may have been part of the passage ritual as well (6:5). The term "anointed one," Messiah in Hebrew and Christ in Greek, came to be applied to Jesus.

Theologically, the primary focus of this text is God's action. God, who does not allow the gift of kingship to be subverted by human rebellion and stubbornness, withdraws the divine Spirit from one ruler and gives it to another (16:13).

David is not chosen because of his outward appearance (although he is described as "handsome" in 16:12). If appearance were the chief criterion Eliab might have been the selection (16:6–7). Instead, narrative suspense is built as Samuel rejects one after the other of Jesse's sons. Finally, David is fingered ("This is he," 6:12). God who sees "the heart" has named one who will follow the word of the Lord and obey God's commandments.

It is instructive to compare God's judgment with human standards for the selection of leaders. In a media age David's "beautiful eyes" and "handsome" features would have carried more weight. We pick candidates for public office who are physically attractive, who come across well on television, who are able to deliver forceful variations of a "canned" speech, and who possess dynamic personalities that move people. No wonder so many of our public figures seem shallow and one-dimensional. We look "on the outward appearance, but the Lord looks on the heart" (6:7).

In this reading and its context we have a recurrence of the Deuteronomic pattern of human failure and divine grace that culminates in the establishment of the monarchy. It is clear in these stories that the monarchy and its kings are a human institution, judged when they fail; however, it is equally clear that kingship was established by God as a channel to fulfill promises made to Israel.

In a way, the history of kingship in Israel resembles a common variation of the game of volleyball. Instead of attempting to score at the expense of others, the point is to keep the ball in the air as long as possible. When someone drops the ball, he or she must leave the game, but the game goes on to the end.

When Saul fails, David is chosen as a representative of God, a man after God's own heart, to safeguard the law and to lead the people in doing the will of God. Because of this divine appointment, and as a result of David's success as a leader, the Davidic line came to be the focal point of future expectation.

One irony of this text is that Saul did not "leave the game." Rather, Saul continued as king for some time beyond the point that God's support for him was withdrawn. The king was not laid to rest with full military honors. No soldiers in tailored uniforms marched beside a horse-drawn caisson. Flags were not flown at half-staff, nor were volleys fired. Saul struggled on with his demons until the moment he fell on his own sword (31:4), while the youth chosen to replace him matured into a capable warrior-leader. In God's eyes his kingship had ended years before, but Saul remained king.

Is not this same dynamic played out in the worlds of business, politics, and the church? Support for the one holding an office is withdrawn, but the person struggles on, sensing a loss of authority, but is unable to acknowledge or face the end. How is a leader to know when the time has come to pass the torch to another? How are Christians to sense the presence or absence of God's Spirit? While it does not address the question directly, this text suggests that (as David's summons came from Samuel) calls to leadership usually come through official representatives and that the presence or absence of God's Spirit be tested by the leader's obedience to God's rule over creation. Is it not generally true that leaders who seize power and who make their own rules are seldom doing the will of God? To focus for preaching: The power to lead normally comes from God through God's appointed representatives and is verified by the faithfulness of the leader to God's rule over creation.

SECOND LESSON: EPHESIANS 5:8–14

The apparent literary interdependence of Colossians and Ephesians has caused some scholars to regard this letter as deutero-Pauline. If Paul is the author, the lack of personal greetings and local references suggests a letter circulated by Tychicus (6:21–22) to a number of churches in Asia Minor, among them the congregation in Ephesus. Specific references to Paul's imprisonment (3:1; 4:1; 6:20) suggest a dating in the early 60s.

The broadest context for understanding this reading is the entire book. In Ephesians 1–3 Paul builds a doctrinal basis for the ethical portion that follows. God's eternal purpose in establishing the church is the backdrop against which the apostle summarizes the good news of the sacrifice, death, and exaltation of Jesus Christ. Particularly in 2:1–22 he focuses on the benefits of Christ for Jew and Gentile alike. Given these benefits Paul goes on in chaps. 4–6 to challenge believers to lead lives worthy of their calling (see 4:1).

A narrower context for interpreting 5:8–14 is Paul's specific appeal to renounce pagan ways in 4:17—5:20. Negatively, the faithful are exhorted to put off the "old nature" belonging to the corrupt world which is passing away (4:22); positively, believers are called to put on the "new nature" created after the likeness of God.

It is clear from the appointed reading that these two natures correspond somehow to the two ages that conjoin in Christ. The writer asserts that "once you were darkness, but now you are light *in the Lord.*" Those who heard this letter read in public worship were creatures, citizens of the world with its attendant darkness. At the same time, by the grace of God (2:8), these very individuals were created anew to be creatures of light and citizens of "the kingdom of Christ and of God" (5:5).

While the preacher will immediately note the contrast and may wish to explore its implications for preaching, there is a danger of oversimplification. Paul calls the baptized to "walk as children of light" (5:8). However, moving from darkness to light in the real world is far more difficult than stepping out of a darkened cinema into a brilliant summer afternoon. Those who accept the gospel in faith continue to live in a dark world even as the enlightening power of God is at work in their lives. As sinners they give in to the evil one; as saints they recognize the power of evil and are given the power to resist temptation and to live in the light (5:11–14).

In this reading indicative statements stand alongside imperative statements and in the closest connection to them. Believers are declared to be "light in the Lord" (v. 8). In v. 15 it is said that "Christ shall give you light." Baptism into Jesus Christ includes believers in a new realm with a new sovereign. At the same time those declared to be light are called to walk as children of light. In chaps. 4–6 this bare-bones challenge is fleshed out. God's claim on us is a part of God's gift to us. Rudolph Bultmann is credited with summarizing the Pauline point in the statement that God calls us to "become what we already are." Light is what Christ both gives and demands.

GOSPEL: JOHN 9:1–41 (OPTION 1)

The Lutheran lectionary appoints this lesson to be read on the Third Sunday in Lent. The Roman Catholic, Episcopal, and Common lectionary all assign the reading to this Fourth Sunday.

The prologue to the Fourth Gospel announced that the Word coming into the world was both life and light (1:1–18). These themes were underscored in John 8 when Jesus proclaimed, "I am the light of the world; he who follows me will not walk in darkness, but will have the light of life" (v. 12). As the raising of Lazarus signifies that Jesus is the source of life (chap. 11), so the healing of the man born blind in this chapter is a sign that Jesus is "the light of the world" (v. 5).

The theme of Jesus as light is a motif associated with the feast of Tabernacles, with the result that the unit does fit in the context provided by the final redactor (see chaps. 7–8). However, commentators feel that chaps. 9–12 may form a tradition that was originally independent and not part of the first draft of the Gospel.[15]

This healing account is as graphic as any in Mark (cf. Mark 7:33; 8:23). In Jesus' day healing powers were attributed to spittle. Apparently, details of the healer's art were suppressed by Matthew and Luke, perhaps in an attempt to spiritualize the miracles. Even in John 5:8 a word is sufficient to bring wholeness. The significance of the water of Siloam is discussed below.

This sixth Johannine sign has literary characteristics similar to its counterparts. Jesus is depicted as acting not out of compassion but as an opportunity for revelation. When the disciples inquire about whose sin caused the man's blindness, his own (prenatally) or his parents, Jesus shifts attention to the opportunity for God to heal (vv. 2, 3).

The confusion attendant to Johannine signs is a prominent characteristic of this narrative. Immediately following the miracle, former neighbors and onlookers wonder if the man healed is the blind man who formerly sat and begged (vv. 8–12). There follow no less than three hearings before the Pharisees, two where the man is interrogated and one where his parents are grilled. With each encounter the Jews become more and more confused and closed to God's revelation. The parents' fear of the Jews and the determination of the leaders to "put out of the synagogue" those who confess Christ (v. 22) reflects the tension of a later time when the Johannine Christians had already been excluded for bearing witness to the name of Christ.

In the final unit of the pericope (vv. 35–41) Jesus confronts the man he healed, who immediately believes in him as the Son of man. In vv. 39–41, a section that reads as if it were added later, the theological implications of blindness and sight are developed. Double meanings abound, with blindness pointing to denial and eyesight the equivalent of faith.

The notion of a causal relationship between sin and sickness was assumed in Jesus' day, despite the protest of the Book of Job. In part, the connection lay in the Hebrew tendency to give God credit for everything good and bad. If an adult suffered, the assumption was that the person's own sin had provoked God's righteous anger. If a child was born with some deformity, the rabbis argued that either the baby sinned while still in the womb or that the iniquity of a previous generation was being visited upon the child by God (Exod. 20:5).

In both the Synoptic Gospels and John, Jesus resists simple connections between sin and sickness (Luke 13:2). In vv. 2 and 3 Jesus is asked about the cause of blindness, but he responds in terms of an opportunity for healing action (see also 11:4). The force of the "we" in v. 4 is to involve Jesus' followers with him in this activity that brings light in a dark world.

At bedside and graveside clergy still shudder to hear axioms, often from the mouths of their own parishioners, that link sin and suffering or blame God for tragedy. "What could you expect, given the life he lived?" "It was meant to be." "It's God's will!" No amount of reasonable rebuttal, especially in the immediate context of suffering, will dislodge this combination of primitive theology and folk wisdom. Suffering makes people feel out of control in what seems to be a chaotic universe. To the frightened person, assigning blame to God makes the inexplicable more reasonable and restores a measure of sanity to a turbulent situation.

The time for apologetic preaching (dialogue with misleading theological assertions) is in proximity to, but somewhat removed from, the immediate trauma. A prominent instance of suffering in the nation, the residential community, or the church family is an opportunity for theological clarification. While the memory lingers, but in the coolness that comes with a little distance from the event, the preacher can assist people to reflect about suffering and its meaning. If the need is apparent in the listeners or the community, this pericope provides an opportunity to address the issue. To summarize: In a situation of suffering, the crucified and risen Christ resists human efforts to assign blame; rather, the Lord seeks opportunities to involve followers in healing activity that will glorify the name of God.

Jesus' directive to wash in the pool has a parallel in Elisha's command to Naaman the leper (2 Kings 5:10–13). Evidently, the water of Siloam (Isa. 8:6) was used in the ceremonies of the feast of Tabernacles. Rabbinic sources mention Siloam as a place of purification.

In the context of Lent, a season committed to preparing candidates for Easter initiation, the connection between baptism and a washing that leads to sight is suggestive for the preacher. While this linkage is not explicit in the text, scholars believe that baptism was practiced in the community of the beloved disciple. For the evangelist the sacraments are a continuation of the power Jesus manifested during his ministry.[17] Having Jesus replace ceremonies of the old covenant with the sacraments of the new may well have been in the mind of the one who crafted this story. For preaching purposes: Baptism leads to enlightenment when persons living in darkness are washed at the command of Jesus, the light of the world.

The confusion of neighbors and those who knew the blind man in his former state as well as the successive interrogations of the healed man and his parents (vv. 8–34) culminate in the healed man's expulsion (v. 34). The sequence of events in the narrative may well reflect the experience of John's own community as it learned, haltingly at first and then more boldly, to confess faith in Jesus Christ. Raymond Brown believes that a group he labels the "crypto-Christians" were allowed to remain in the synagogue with both a low profile (keeping their beliefs quiet) and a low Christology. Apparently, their view of Jesus ended where the conviction of the blind man began, "He is a prophet" (v. 17). Brown asserts: "The blind man is acting out the history of the Johannine community, a community that would have had little tolerance for others who refused to make the difficult choice that they had to make."[18] In the view of the evangelist, by not taking a public stand on Jesus' behalf, those who remained in the synagogue were showing they did not believe in him.

In an age when it is thought odd or gauche to bring faith convictions into public discourse, those who call themselves members of the Christian community and those preparing for membership are instructed by this reading to witness boldly for Christ. As he did to the blind man, Jesus challenges those who are healed in the waters of baptism today to confess publicly their faith in the healer.

The religious leaders in this lection are a blatant example of how closed some can become to the gospel. They did their best both to label Jesus a sinner ("working" on the Sabbath) and to deny the identity of the blind man in order to discredit the miracle. Even his parents were interrogated to establish the identity of the former blind man (vv. 18–23). By his second interview it is clear that the Pharisees have made up their minds about Jesus. However, the new believer is not intimidated; he argues that only one "from God" can do miracles. For this testimony the rulers label him a sinner and cast him out (v. 34).

Clearly, Jesus was a threat to the religious leaders of his day. On a scale ranging from flexibility to rigidity the Pharisees were rigid. Their fixed categories did not permit them to include a prophet without a pedigree (v. 29). As experts in the law their identities were wrapped up with Moses the lawgiver (vv. 28–29), whose authority seemed challenged by this upstart. The healed man struggled to "see" who Jesus was; the rulers sought ways to deny what their eyes told them. Their biases interfered with their perceptions, and the sighted Pharisees became closed (blind).

Clergy deal with rigid, closed-minded persons daily; indeed, some clergy are afflicted with the same disease. It will be tempting in constructing a sermon to focus the searchlight of this text on those outside the family of faith who are blind to Christ. Yet the point of this text is that Jesus encountered resistance and was rejected, not by "outsiders" (the blind man) but by the leaders of the very community that should have received him gladly. A study of the psychological dynamics of resistance and closedness is essential for pastors, not just for preaching this text, but for dealing with the Pharisee in the church and in ourselves.

A sermon of contrast is suggested by vv. 39–41, which summarize the message of the entire text. People who claim to be objective about life still insist that "seeing is believing." In a scientific age we hear people repeat the axiom as if it were true in all cases. Rational people argue that hard evidence is essential to decision making. This text makes a contrary point, that under certain circumstances "believing is seeing." Faith leads to sight. The story of the blind man and the Pharisees can be cited as evidence for both terms of the contrast. The demand for proof closes people to Jesus and leads to rejection; God's gift of faith leads to spiritual sight.

GOSPEL: MATTHEW 20:17–28 (OPTION 2)

The reading is divided into two or three parts. On the road to Jerusalem Jesus foretells his passion for the third time (vv. 17–19). The story of the mother of James and John asking for a place of honor for her sons and a discussion about drinking the cup (vv. 20–24) follow. Sayings about the nature of servanthood complete this unit in Matthew's Gospel (vv. 25–28), although these axioms may have circulated independently in the oral tradition.

The entire unit appears to be dependent upon Mark 10:32–45. While any of the three parts could be preached alone, to do so would miss the marvelous unity achieved by Mark's linkage. Particularly challenging for contemporary listeners is the contrast between power as understood by Jesus and power as sought by the Zebedees.

The mother of James and John was asking, What's in it for my sons? In today's person-centered culture the question seems entirely relevant. Even Christians speak glibly about "looking out for number one." Young people choose life-styles on the basis of how they feel, not whether they are right or helpful. The career tracks of many people control their decision making and their entire lives. They will know at any given moment where they are on the ladder of success. Even persons willing to volunteer for community projects wonder if their names will be mentioned in the newspapers. We are never far from the bottom-line question, What's in it for me?

Apparently, Jesus' disciples had begun to question the rewards of service. They had been nobodies all their lives, poor fishermen and tradesmen, shoved around and seldom taken seriously. They had spent years on the road, organizing rallies by day and often camping under the stars at night. While Jesus' name was on everyone's lips, even the inner circle of the disciples remained nameless and faceless. As Jerusalem came into view, and it seemed as if Jesus might be swept into power by popular acclaim, Mom Zebedee wanted some of that power for her boys. "Command that these two sons of mine may sit, one at your right hand and one at your left, in your kingdom" (17:21).

Yet the sort of power the Zebedees wanted was no power at all compared to what Jesus offered. What Jesus held out to those who followed him was the power of weakness. Jesus was on his way to Jerusalem, not to rule but to die. He offered only the antagonism of the authorities, a cross outside the city, and the cold dampness of Joseph's tomb. His was a different formula for success. Jesus sought service rather than position. Jesus' reply to the two disciples (not to their mother) indicated that they had misunderstood. Their reward would not be what they could get but what they could become—servants. "Whoever would be great among you must be your servant, and whoever would be first among you must be your slave; even as the Son of man came not to be served but to serve, and to give his life as a ransom for many" (20:26–28).

The question "Are you able?" and the response "We are able" frames the dominant cup image in v. 22. Play a word association game and some interesting connections emerge. One group of laity, who studied this passage, listed: loving cup, a trophy of achievement; demitasse, a cup of after-dinner coffee; "my cup runneth over" from Psalm 23; the king's cup, a mark of royalty; the coffee mug that marks a break from work; a measuring cup; to cup the hand when drinking from a stream; the disposable paper cup of our throw-away society; the communion chalice; tin cup, symbolic of poverty or need; the cup Jesus shared with his disciples in the Upper Room.

In Matthew 20 Jesus used the cup as an image of suffering and death, but James and John, who yearned to rule at Jesus' right and left, took the cup as an image of authority and power. Pridefully, they pronounced themselves able to drain the vessel without understanding the implications of their boast. What do our cup associations say about us and our lives? Are we better able than James and John to hear Jesus' call to servanthood? To focus: Jesus warns ambitious (and confused) disciples that rank in the kingdom is a gift to those able to drink the cup of service and suffering.

The Fifth Sunday in Lent

Lutheran	Roman Catholic	Episcopal	Common Lectionary
Ezek. 37:1–3, 11–14	Ezek. 37:12–14	Ezek. 37:1–3, 11–14	Ezek. 37:1–14
Rom. 8:11–19	Rom. 8:8–11	Rom. 6:16–23	Rom. 8:6–11
John 11:1–53	John 11:1–45	John 11:18–44	John 11:(1–16) 17–45

What Ezekiel proclaimed to "dead" exiles, and what the Fourth Gospel asserts through the sign of Lazarus, is that God gives life to the dead. Paul reaffirms that God's action of raising Jesus from the dead is the basis of both present and future life for believers (Romans 8).

FIRST LESSON: EZEKIEL 37:1–3, 11–14

Internal evidence (1:1–3; 28:17) places Ezekiel's prophetic activity between 594 and 571 B.C. A son of Busi and a priest in the Jerusalem temple,
Ezekiel was called to be a prophet when he was about thirty.

Ezekiel was a prophet of the exile. When Josiah's son Jehoiakim, a
vassal of Babylon, began acting independently (602 B.C.), Nebuchadrezzar
beseiged Jerusalem (598 B.C.). After several months the defenders capit-
ulated. The palace and temple were plundered. Ezekiel was deported along
with the new king, Jehoiakim's son Jehoiachin (eighteen years old), the
royal family, and members of the upper and artisan classes. While some
prophets predicted a brief period of bondage to be followed by a speedy
return, Ezekiel angered many by anticipating an extended sentence as a
result of God's judgment.

Jerusalem was not destroyed in 598 B.C. Judah continued as a semi-
independent state under Jehoiachin's uncle, Zedekiah, who was soon engaged in subterfuge. Hoping for Egyptian support, Zedekiah moved toward
an open break with Babylon (17:15). Ezekiel condemned this action. His
oracles of judgment upon Israel (chaps. 1–24) were intended to alert his
people, both at home and in exile, to the futility of this course. Ezekiel's
prophecies of judgment on foreign nations are collected in chaps. 25–32.
There is a tendency among scholars to see the harshness and violence of
Ezekiel's language in all of these oracles as evidence of his intensity of
feeling for his people's fate and his burning sense of the holiness of God.

When the holy city was destroyed (587 B.C.), the temple burned, and
the royal household executed (2 Kings 25:8), the prophet envisioned his
task as assisting the exiles to preserve their identity as Yahweh's covenant
people in preparation for God's liberation of them. This reading from chap.
37 appears amid a collection (chaps. 33–48) that Walter Eichrodt labels
"portrayals of the time of salvation." [19] These oracles of hope, designed
to uplift a despairing people, conclude Ezekiel's prophetic activity and
were placed, by the prophet or by an editor, at the end of the book.

This oracle (37:1–10) takes the form of a vision. The formula used to
introduce the vision (v. 1) is stereotypical and suggests how the word of
God came to the prophet who had been selected to proclaim it. The prophet
is transported to the valley-plain (v. 2), the southern Tigris-Euphrates valley
near the Babylonian canal, Chebar (see 1:1, 3:22). The term "son of man"
(v. 3) suggests the weakness and lowliness of a human being in the presence
of the power and glory of Israel's God. When asked if the bones can come

to life, Ezekiel made no claim for human power but deferred to God who alone can bring the dead to life. The heart of the vision (vv. 5–9) is the resuscitation of the dry bones by the Spirit and word of God as spoken through the prophet.

Dead bones coming to life is a striking image to enliven proclamation. Listeners unfamiliar with Ezekiel 37 may have a mental picture of the miracle from the spiritual "Dry Bones." The word "coma" with its attendant image of deep and prolonged unconsciousness or stupor may suggest to contemporary listeners the living death of Israel and the church. Preachers have also used the anatomical image of "amputation" to suggest the separation felt by exiles between themselves, their land, and God.

To preach this text as a precursor of either the resurrection of Jesus from the dead or the resurrection of individual believers at the end of the age would not be true either to the present tense or to the corporate focus of the passage. While Ezekiel's vision pictures a resuscitation of the bones of dead human beings, the interpretation of the vision (37:11–14) centers on the imminent energizing of a despairing people who feel cut off from God. The vision celebrates the power of Yahweh to restore the dead to life; that is, to create a new Israel to replace this "dead" nation of exiles.

This means, of course, that it would be incongruous for the preacher to highlight anecdotes of *individuals* into whose bodies God has breathed new life. While depression with its chronic sadness and hopelessness is an apt metaphor for the condition that beset Israel, the preacher should bring the message of the text to focus on the contemporary *people* of God, the Christian church.

Laity and clergy, who tend to view today's church as hopeless and lifeless, should resonate with the plaintive cry of the exiles ("Our bones are dried up, and our hope is lost; we are clean cut off"), as well as with the message of life ("I will open your graves, and raise you from your graves, O my people"). Individual congregations may experience hopelessness and lifelessness in declining attendance, loss of leadership, or blunted mission. Isolation ("clean cut off") is a common experience in the midst of religious, racial, or ethnic change in neighborhoods. Of course, the good news (God's shock therapy) can be targeted to match specific examples of despair or isolation. A theological summary of the essential message of this sermon might read: In a situation of despair God proclaims the good news of life from death, so that a hopeful church may testify to the greatness and power of God.

In linking Israel's situation to that of contemporary despairing nations, the preacher should be restrained in evoking images of prison camps, special garb, dungeons, solitary confinement, or torture. Stories of present-day hostages, while gaining listener attention and adding spice to the sermon, do not parallel Israel's situation. While most of the Hebrews in Babylon were serfs of the government, tilling the land to which they were assigned, they were not confined under guard and were free to worship as they pleased. The situation today of black people in South Africa is a more reasonable analogy to the plight of the exiles. Being confined to particular neighborhoods or excluded from living in others for reasons of race or religion is not legal in the United States; yet, in practice, minority groups continue to experience such in subtle forms (e.g., "redlining" in real estate).

A greater challenge for the preacher is to explore ways in which the contemporary church is in bondage and to provide specific examples of how a liberating gospel can evoke hope. Many congregations seem bound to self-serving behavior that leads to institutional and spiritual death. How often we hear the expression, "We always do it this way here." It is clear from this text that for Israel the message of life did *not* mean a mere resumption of the past. The rebellious nation had to die for the genuinely new people to be born, and this death to life transformation was possible only as a miracle and gift of God. In sum: The Lord alone is able to liberate the church, captive to its own selfish and ineffective patterns, for a ministry of faithfulness to the will of God.

Ezekiel 37 gives the preacher an opportunity to highlight the *means* by which the gift of life is given. God employs a vision to communicate with the prophet, but Ezekiel himself becomes a channel for God's word of life ("Therefore prophesy, and say to them, Thus says the Lord God," v. 12). This text would be an effective vehicle for proclamation on the occasion or on the anniversary of the ordination of a pastor or at the commissioning of lay evangelists and parish visitors.

Breath/wind/spirit is a source of life in the passage, and it may be tempting to explore apparent New Testament parallels. However, analogies to Pentecost might seem anachronistic to believers who are keyed to the context and mood of Lent. Pentecost marked a climactic energizing of a despairing church by the Holy Spirit of the risen Christ. The miracle envisioned in Ezekiel 37 is the revivification of Babylonian exiles by Yahweh over a period of time. The dramatic summoning of breath from the four winds

(Ezekiel's "gift of the spirit" in vv. 9–10) rests on the ancient Hebrew notion that life comes as an infusion of the breath of God. Christians believe that life comes to the church today as the gospel is proclaimed and the Holy Spirit evokes a response of faith in Jesus the Christ. In sum: Through the word of God contemporary prophets announce the good news of life from death, so that a Spirit-filled church may witness to the risen Lord's greatness and power.

We should be careful not to stress Yahweh's love and compassion as a motive for a gracious approach to people feeling isolated, abandoned, or cut off. While God's covenant love is testified to elsewhere in the Old Testament, the prophet's assignment here is to proclaim the name of God which has been profaned by the unfaithfulness of Israel. God's action in saving a people who had broken covenant is ultimately for the sake of the honor of the divine name among the nations of the world (37:28). We must now inquire whether the ineffectiveness of today's church and our own individual congregations has profaned the name of God in the midst of a secular culture. The good news for the exiles was that even in Babylon the Lord was able to intervene and rescue the people, so that the nations would know God's power and glory. To a church that feels abandoned in a secular society, God comes in the word, calling the despairing into fellowship and renewing the church, so that the life-giving power of the Lord is proclaimed to all.

SECOND LESSON: ROMANS 8:(6–11) 11–19

The link between all of today's readings is Rom. 8:11. Here Paul reaffirms what Ezekiel assured "dead" exiles and what John proclaimed through the sign of Lazarus, namely, that God gives life to the dead. God's action of raising Jesus from the grave is the basis of both present and future hope for believers. In Paul's theology as exhibited in Romans, life for the faithful begins with justification and extends to the resurrection of the dead. If the Spirit of God who raised Jesus from the grave (Rom. 4:24) lives in believers, then life will be both an immediate and future gift of the Spirit.

Whether or not verses from Rom. 8:1–10 are read in public worship, they are essential for an understanding of the verses that follow. In 8:1–4 Paul links God's saving action in Jesus Christ to the believer's life in the Spirit of Christ. In 8:4–11 the apostle asserts that as the law and sin lead to death so the Spirit leads to life.

The contrast between life "according to the flesh" which leads to death, and life "according to the Spirit" which results in life and peace (v. 6), must be clear to preacher and listeners. Paul occasionally uses the term "flesh" to mean corporal existence ("sending his own Son in the likeness of sinful flesh," 8:3); more often the "fleshly" life identifies a life of sin, a life focused on pleasing the self. For more detail on 8:1–10 see the Fourth Sunday in Lent, second lesson.

The good news is that believers who received the Spirit in baptism will be aided to "put to death the deeds of the body" (8:13). In Lent, a season whose lections stress baptismal renewal, the preacher may well highlight the gift of baptismal dying and rising with Christ.

However, what God gives in baptism is what God demands from the baptized (6:1–14). The counterpoint of the good news of the life-giving Spirit is a clear call for believers to live the Spirit-filled life. Grammatically speaking, it is the indicative, the fact of God's life-giving action, that precedes and forms the basis of the imperative of God's call to live in the Spirit. The Pauline rhythm of God's action preceding and enabling human response is a clue to structuring a sermon with two major plot moves. The life-giving Spirit of God, who raised Jesus from the dead, enables and challenges believers to renounce a self-serving life and live a Spirit-filled life.

A sermon built on the contrast between fleshly life and Spirit-filled life is suggested by vv. 12–15, a message both challenging and insightful in this age of the individual.

The appropriate response to God's gift of life is to live as children of God (v. 14).

In texts like Romans 8, which abound with masculine language (e.g., "sons" and "sonship"), we can indicate sensitivity to the feelings of listeners by paraphrasing the Greek text (e.g., "sons and daughters of God") and by stressing the text's own inclusive terms ("children"). To focus: In the face of a culture marked by self-serving individualism, God calls believers to a Spirit-led life centered on God and God's children.

The role of the Spirit in the prayer and worship life of the community is another aspect of this reading (vv. 15–16). Whether ecstatic prayer or the Lord's Prayer is intended in v. 15, it is the Spirit praying in and through us who convinces us that we are God's children. To summarize: God's people experience the activity of the Spirit in corporate worship.

Suffering is a reality of life for Christians also (8:18–25). Putting to death the deeds of the flesh is a constant struggle for individual believers. Flesh and Spirit contend, temptations are everywhere, and Christians are called to make hard choices in the hostile environment of a self-centered age.

In Paul's writings there is a strong correlation between life in the Spirit and persecution. The congregation in Rome had experienced the animosity of unbelievers and some repression from the government prior to Paul's letter, although when Romans was written, the age of Christians going to the lions was years in the future. Believers today who advocate justice for the poor, the sick, minorities, and other oppressed persons are likely to suffer hostility and resentment. The reality of present suffering, suffering with Christ (v. 17), precedes the glory to be revealed. However, in this passage the hope of glory is the key to endurance. It may be more effective for a sermon to begin with and build upon the good news of hope. For example: The hope of glory enables despairing believers to endure the sufferings attendant to a Spirit-filled life in a fleshly world.

GOSPEL: JOHN 11:1–53

The story of the raising of Lazarus is set by the evangelist at a crucial place in the last days of Jesus' earthly ministry. For the writer of John, the sensation created by this miracle on Jesus' final journey to Jerusalem precipitates the chain of events that lead to Jesus' death.

The literary context of the miracle in John, between the winter feast of Dedication (10:22) and the spring feast of Passover (13:1), suggests an unlikely scenario of three quick trips to Jerusalem and its environs within the space of three to four months. The synoptic chronology of a single trip to Jerusalem, with Bethany as a place of lodging for Jesus' traveling party, receives more support from scholars. Raymond E. Brown suggests that at one stage in the formation of the Fourth Gospel the public ministry of Jesus ended with what is now 10:40–42 and that chaps. 11 and 12 are a later insertion into the Gospel.[20] Supporting this thesis is the fact that in these two chapters "the Jews" seem to be ordinary people sympathetic to Jesus and his ministry, while elsewhere in the Gospel "the Jews" are hostile religious authorities.

The authenticity of these chapters is called into question even more by the surprising fact that the Synoptics seem to know nothing of Lazarus, a friend of Jesus. Some suggest that chap. 11 is a composition based primarily on Lucan material, the raising of the son of the widow of Nain (7:11–16), the Lucan story of the beggar Lazarus (16:19–31), and the story of Mary and Martha (10:38–42). However, it is equally possible that both Luke and John were influenced by oral tradition about how Jesus raised a friend from death.

In the Synoptics the cleansing of the temple leads to the Sanhedrin's decision to do away with Jesus (see 2:13–25 for the Johannine chronology), but the evangelist is creative in making this miracle the precipitating cause of Jesus' death, provoking a session of the Sanhedrin (11:46–53), which determines to kill him. The evangelist employs this culminating miracle, the sign of Jesus' power over death, as the seventh and ultimate sign to which the only responses are offense (by the religious leaders) or faith (by "many of the Jews," v. 45). Structurally, chaps. 11 and 12 conclude the Book of Signs and serve as a transition to the Book of Glory. Jesus' public ministry comes to an end, and Jesus' passion begins.

As were Martha and Mary, listeners may be disturbed at Jesus' delay in coming to the aid of a beloved friend (v. 4). In John's Gospel, however, signs are occasions of revelation rather than narratives of compassion. And while v. 5 does seem intended to underscore Jesus' concern for Lazarus (the verb used is *agapaō*), the preacher may choose to highlight the paradox of love mingled with seeming indifference as a point of connection with the reaction of sensitive worshipers.

In fact, the Johannine Jesus typically works according to his own time-table and not according to the urgent prompting of others. Here the sisters summon him to Bethany, and he delays; the disciples initially resist going, but Jesus announces his departure (vv. 11, 12).

Actually, the "delay" is enhanced dramatically to make the point that Lazarus was dead and that the resuscitation is a miracle–sign. Martha's protest about an "odor" (v. 39) has the same effect. Apparently it was an opinion among the rabbis that the soul hovered near the body for three days. By Jesus' arrival on the fourth day (v. 17), the only hope of restoring Lazarus to life lay in the one who proclaimed himself "the resurrection." Likewise, our only hope of life beyond death is the promise contained in v. 25. We may summarize the Johannine understanding that Jesus is already victorious when he is "lifted up" on the cross: For believers, hope for life beyond death for themselves and loved ones rests entirely in Jesus who on the cross won the victory over sin and death.

For the evangelist, new life in the present age is a related gift of Jesus. In the face of death the Jesus of the Fourth Gospel asserts, "I am the resurrection *and the life*" (v. 25). Christians accustomed to hearing those words at the grave sites of loved ones may hear only the good news of resurrection in this lesson. But for the writer of John, much of what is expected on Resurrection Day has been accomplished already. In baptism, in the community of believers, life is a present reality for followers of Jesus Christ. "Eternal life begins, not at the funeral home and not at the end of time, but with him."[21] His dead friend bursting from the cave with bandages flapping prefigures both the Easter miracle of Jesus' own resurrection and life with Christ here and now. Believers who die physically will live spiritually (v. 25); believers who are alive spiritually will never die spiritually (v. 26).

The "community of the beloved disciple," expelled from the synagogue and faced with persecution by "the Jews," would have heard this gospel gladly.[22] Each day was a struggle to sustain faith in the crucified and risen Lord amidst tension, hostility, and harassment. While faith may be initiated as a climactic event, the experience of Christians is that faith is renewed daily as struggling people trust in the promises of the gospel. This can easily be made specific: To sufferers who believe the sign of Lazarus, Jesus renews faith and gives life in the midst of _____(specify the loss). We should feel confident targeting this good news to losses of different kinds (e.g., death of a family member, loss of job, divorce).

Listeners may be confused that formal mourning seems to follow rather than precede burial. In Israel (as in many tropical climates today) burial was on the day of death, without embalming, and a thirty-day period of mourning followed. Jesus' open expression of grief, while not a major motif in the story, is something of a corrective for persons in our death-denying and grief-restricting culture (vv. 33–38). The example of Jesus, who was moved to weep at the death of his friend, encourages us to express our grief at the loss of loved ones.

The evangelist's timing of the sign of Lazarus is more theological than chronological, a fact that becomes evident in the final unit of the pericope (vv. 45–53). The Synoptic Gospels do not seem to know about a session of the council weeks prior to Passover, although Matt. 26:3–5 records one just two days prior. In the Fourth Gospel the council is convened in response to the Lazarus miracle, and members of the Sanhedrin express anxiety about Jesus' signs. The bill of indictment collates charges made elsewhere in the Gospel (v. 48). As the centerpiece of this unit, Caiaphas, the high priest, predicts unwittingly that one person should die for the nation, and not for the nation only but for God's scattered children. The preacher will wish to be alert to contemporary instances of hostile authorities giving unwitting testimony to the life-giving power of the gospel. From time to time, examples are found in the reports of church leaders who journey to countries where for some years communist governments repressed Christianity, but where the church presently is flourishing.

One should not read the words of Caiaphas in support of "universalism" (all will be saved). In the evangelist's scheme, the hostile "world" (including but not limited to "the Jews") would not be included in God's scattered children. Presumably, Gentiles who believe in Jesus are to be gathered with dispersed Jews. Under the sign of Lazarus, Jesus goes to his cross as one whose death brings life to God's children (believers) in many places. A sermon incorporating these ideas can contain the message: God uses even enemies of the gospel to proclaim that Christ died to give life to all who believe, wherever they may be.

Should the preacher desire to utilize the entire pericope (11:1–53), the dilemma of the sign of Lazarus for those who would believe is a unifying theme for preaching. In the Fourth Gospel the coming of the Son calls women and men to decision. Those who believe are not condemned, but those who deny are condemned already (3:17–21). In this chapter affirmations of believers range from titles suggesting superficial respect (Rabbi) to the profoundly insightful (Christ, the Son of God). Today, too, persons invest Jesus with various degrees of authority and find titles to express their levels of commitment. The preacher should be attentive to terminology in the media. Beyond the matter of titles, signs are occasions of revelation in John, and the narratives typically include the response of participants. Some see and believe ("many of the Jews," v. 45); others become blind and deny (the Pharisees). Note that the issue is not the authenticity or historicity of this particular event but the response of people to Jesus, who claims power over death. In sum: The raising of Lazarus, a sign of Jesus' power to give life now and beyond death, confronts contemporary listeners with a response of offense or faith.

Notes

1. F. Scott Fitzgerald, *The Great Gatsby* (1925; New York: Macmillan Co., 1980), 182.

2. Eduard Schweizer, *The Good News according to Matthew,* trans. David E. Green (Atlanta: John Knox Press, 1975), 141ff.

3. Ibid., 60.

4. Ibid., 58.

5. Eduard Schweizer, *The Good News according to Luke,* trans. David E. Green (Atlanta: John Knox Press, 1984), 82.

6. Alvin Toffler, *Future Shock* (New York: Bantam, 1971), 377–82.

7. Robert E. C. Browne, The *Ministry of the Word* (Philadelphia: Fortress Press, 1976), 84.

8. Raymond E. Brown, *The Gospel according to John I–XII,* Anchor Bible (Garden City, N.Y.: Doubleday & Co., 1966), 136.

9. Claus Westermann, *Isaiah 40–66* (Philadelphia: Westminster Press, 1969), 105.

10. Douglas John Hall, *God and Human Suffering* (Minneapolis: Augsburg Publishing House, 1986), 145.

11. Ernst Haenchen, *John 1* (Philadelphia: Fortress Press, 1984), 231ff.

12. Ibid., 219.

13. While a woman figured prominently in the source narrative, it is clear that the evangelist himself highlighted the roles of women as leaders. See Raymond E. Brown, *Community of the Beloved Disciple* (Paramus, N.J.: Paulist Press, 1979), 183ff.

14. *Aboth Rabbi Nathan* 2 (1d), cited from Haenchen, *John 1,* 224.

15. Ernst Haenchen, *John 2* (Philadelphia: Fortress Press, 1984), 37.

16. Brown, *John I–XII,* 372.

17. Brown, *Community of the Beloved Disciple,* 88.

18. Ibid., 72.

19. W. Eichrodt, *Ezekiel* (Philadelphia: Westminster Press, 1970).

20. Brown, *John I–XII,* 427ff.

21. Fred B. Craddock, *The Gospels* (Nashville: Abingdon Press, 1981), 138.

22. A thesis of Brown's, elaborated in *Community of the Beloved Disciple.*